INTRODUCTION

Oh, dear: who doesn't groan when Derek from Accounts puts that notice up above the water-cooler. 'You don't have to be mad to work here, but it helps.' And there's nothing more cringe-making than when someone recounts a story they promise is 'totally crazy and completely wacky', and it turns out to be rather less wondrous than the sight of drying emulsion.

So, clearly, I take my credibility into my own hands when I promise you a book choc-full of mad cars.

What I think I can guarantee, however, is a compendium of left-field motor cars the like of which you will not have seen gathered together before. You can read about forty of the weirdest machines from the motoring world described in detail. Find out why and how they came into being and what makes them, in my possibly twisted and biased opinion, rather mad.

And then enjoy, if that's the right word, ten categorised chapters on mad cars that have one major thing in common but are, otherwise, extremely barmy. Whether you like off-road cars, three-wheelers or even cars you can make at home, I hope there is something here to raise an eyebrow.

Sadly, however, the era of the mad car – the strange designs, the colourful characters, the warped plans – is sliding to a gradual halt. More than nine out of ten cars around the world today are made by just ten huge corporations – important companies in which there is no place for cars that don't conform. For instance, the VW Golf, Skoda Octavia, Audi TT and Audi A3 might all look different but they share an identical 'platform' which has been engineered for myriad uses. It is, of course, excellent but it's this homogenisation that is gradually making the car world a duller place.

It is for our own good, of course. New cars are safer, more environment friendly and better made than ever before. The price we pay, however, is that there will never be another Hudson Commodore, Steyr-Puch Haflinger or, possibly, Nissan Pao again. With so few car makers, all of them geared up for battle with one another, is there a place any longer for independent designers like William Towns or John Weitz, and will determined people like Norah Docker, Nubar Gulbenkian and Boris Forter ever be able to create their own, albeit odd, motoring dreams any more?

Anyway, *Mad Cars* exists purely for your reading pleasure, and please feel free let to me know what you think about it: you can send me an e-mail at chapman.media@virgin.net. However, there are two reasons why it's been possible to put the book together. First, the pictures, all of which come from my collection. Because many have been kindly given to me over the years by car manufacturers and public relations people, I would like to thank them collectively. And second, my wife, without whose help *Mad Cars* would never have got written on time. I dedicate it to the baby she's been carrying throughout its genesis. I don't know what model it is yet but all I can say is: 'You don't have to be mad to live here but. . .'.

Giles Chapman

THE ASTON MARTIN
DBS V8 BY OGLE IN
DETAIL

Built: 1972 in Newport
Pagnell,
Buckinghamshire and
Letchworth,
Hertfordshire
Engine: V8, 5340cc
Top speed: unknown
Sold in the UK? No
Number made: 2

LIGHTING-UP TIME HAD A NEW MEANING WITH THIS GLAZED GLAMOURPUSS

'This must be just about the most desirable object ever produced by the British motor industry,' said Raymond Baxter on BBC1's *Tomorrow's World* in 1972. 'It's a beautiful piece of design.' This was music to the ears of Tom Karen and his team at Ogle Design. After all, ripping the body off an Aston Martin DBS V8 and trying to replace it with an even more dramatic one would never be easy.

CLEVEREST
FEATURES

OUT OF 10

1st

The car's glass was attached to its outer structure, while gold strips in the roof kept the harsh rays of the sun at bay.

With its distinctive, wedge-shaped profile and classic GT proportions, Ogle's Aston Martin DBS was quite the head-turner.

MAD for it!

At the time this was British supercar design at its cutting-edge best, with a shape later copied for cars like the TVR Tasmin. The glass roof was also a style-setter for today's models, even if the trademark rear lights never caught on.

SAD for it! But for a sponsor with more money than sense this flight of fancy would never have seen the light of day. Not that you could link baccy and brake-horsepower together like this now – the anti-smoking lobby would be down on you like a ton of glass ashtrays.

Tobacco company Wills commissioned Ogle to build a unique car to help launch a new brand of cigarettes. The resulting Aston-based sports car had a dramatic wedge profile, raised tail and a Triplex Sundym all-glass roof with built-in heating element and special gold strips to deflect strong sunlight. 'I was quite proud of it', recalls Karen. 'Until then, no-one else had stuck glass on to the outside of a car to give it a completely glazed effect.'

A very rare moment captured: the two Ogle DBSs photographed together in the early 1970s, the blue original and the red replica – happily, both still exist.

One of the 'Sotheby Special's most striking features was its two rows of rear lights, 22 in total – the more brake lights were on, the harder the car was braking.

But its most remarkable feature was two rows of eleven rear lights that worked sequentially: four indicators, two reversing lights and two reflectors, and ten brake lights of which the three nearest the 'corners' of the cars were brighter to show followers how progressive the braking was. They were a safety aid, says Karen, but also very dramatic.

The 'Sotheby Special' was first shown at the 1972 Montreal Motor Show in dark blue picked out with gold coachlines – just like the fag packets. Sotheby cigarettes were a flop, but one other Ogle Aston was ordered by a wealthy Buckinghamshire woman and painted a claret-red. Both still survive.

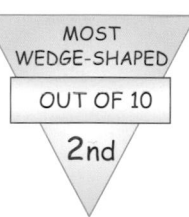

MOST WEDGE-SHAPED
OUT OF 10
2nd

THE AVANTI IN DETAIL

Built: 1965–91 in South Bend, Indiana and Youngstown, Ohio, USA
Engine: V8, 5360/5735/6555/4998cc
Top speed: 140mph
Sold in the UK? No
Number made: 3,000 approx.

HOW NATHAN AND LEO KEPT AN AMERICAN DESIGN CLASSIC ALIVE

America's Avanti almost matched our own Morgan for venerability. Vaunted in 1962 when it was announced by Studebaker, the car was still theoretically available twenty-nine years on. Its father, Raymond Loewy, however, had become accustomed to his work attaining immortality by the time he died in 1986. The man who virtually invented industrial design single-handedly – when he stylishly clad the Gestetner duplicating machine – is outlived by his classic Coca-Cola bottle, the Lucky Strike cigarette pack and NASA's Skylab interior.

MOST ATTRACTIVE

OUT OF 10

1st

A classic shape, preserved in aspic: this is a 1985 example of the Avanti, little changed from the 1963 car that had been a credit to Raymond Loewy's design genius.

Here is a 1989 Avanti, on which the modification fairies have been weaving their dodgy magic – the airdam, sideskirts and modern wheels don't add anything to those famous lines.

His sharp and unadorned lines for the glassfibre-bodied, supercharged V8 Avanti were instantly hailed by a country weaned on Detroit's steel behemoths.

Unfortunately, Studebaker itself was bankrupt by 1964 but two of its dealers, Nathan Altman and Leo Newman, bought the old Indiana factory and continued to hand-make around 100 Avanti IIs each year. The Studebaker engine was replaced by powerful V8s borrowed from the Chevrolet Corvette. Although the enterprise subsequently changed hands twice, the car continued to be available until 1991, latterly also as a convertible, a four-door saloon and even a stretched limousine – if you really still wanted one.

As its car-crazy designer, Loewy would have been chuffed.

MAD for it! For decades the Avanti was as close as America got to a living classic sports car legend in the mould of Britain's Morgan, and keeping it alive meant more people could appreciate Raymond Loewy's masterful styling.

 SAD for it! What was all the fuss about? The Studebaker Avanti wasn't a bad looker when the Beatles were still a spotty pub band, but it didn't merit being kept alive for three decades; only eccentrics would have bought one instead of a Porsche in 1991.

Avanti sponsored the 1989 Palm Springs Vintage GP and Concours d'Elegance, hence the old single seater, but slicing the car's roof off probably added more glamour to the venerable marque.

THE BENTLEY T-SERIES
BY PININFARINA IN
DETAIL

Built: 1968 in Crewe, Cheshire, UK and Turin, Italy
Engine: V8, 6230cc
Top speed: unknown
Sold in the UK? No
Number made: 1

HANSON IS AS HANSON DOES . . . IN A WILD ONE-OFF BENTLEY

Lord Hanson, the Yorkshire-born tycoon, built Hanson plc into one of the UK's most successful industrial conglomerates with his late partner Lord White. But he wasn't always part of the establishment. Just as he got up the noses of industry rivals with his audacious business deals, so he doubtless ruffled a few feathers at Rolls-Royce.

MOST ATTRACTIVE
OUT OF 10
2nd

MAD for it!

When you're rich enough to buy a concept car and use it as your everyday set of wheels, then you know you've arrived. It's just a pity this chic coupé stayed unique while the heavy-handed Camargue went on sale.

The funky oblong headlights sit surprisingly well with the bluff Bentley radiator grille on the front of Pininfarina's T-Series, but a production car it was not to be.

The suave, clean-lined profile that captured Lord Hanson's heart; Pininfarina would later style the Camargue, a much clumsier design in almost every way.

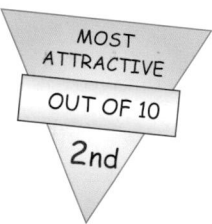

The four round rear lights are a real Ferrari touch, but there's still plenty of room in the boot for anything from shotguns to golfbags.

Not for him any old common or garden Bentley: when Hanson caught sight of the sleek show car that Italian coachbuilder Pininfarina created in 1968 based on a Bentley T-Series, he knew his name was written all over it.

Quite apart from the Ferrari-like sloping roof, oblong headlamps and leather (rather than walnut) facia, the car did away with a 'flying B' bonnet mascot. Terribly non-U, old boy.

It was this car that inspired the later and much uglier Rolls-Royce Camargue – a car that divided Rolls staff themselves into lovers and loathers. Our captain of industry, meanwhile, loved this one-off T-Series, covering almost 15,000 miles in it before selling the unique Bentley in 1979. At £225,000 at the time, the press christened it the most expensive used car ever – an epithet that probably made the shrewd Hanson chuckle.

Probably one of the best-looking Bentleys of the 1960s, the Pininfarina T once changed hands for £225,000, making it one heck of a 'used car'.

SAD for it! Bentleys are British and should stay that way. Mixing their bulldog character with Italian design can make for an uncomfortable mixture, and while this car may have suited a maverick peer, it was always going to be a mongrel in the marque's glorious bloodline.

Er, well, possibly the less said about the Camargue the better, and this US-bound example has not exactly been improved with white details by Hooper's coachpainters.

The 1991 Bentley Continental R finally brought the concept of a sexy-looking Bentley coupé back to life, and proved to be a successful car right round the world.

CHITTY CHITTY BANG BANG IN DETAIL

Built: 1967 in Hertfordshire
Engine: V6, 2994cc
Top speed: unknown
Sold in the UK? No
Number made: 1

CHITTY CHITTY BANG BANG, OUR FINE FOUR-FENDERED FRIEND

Count Louis Zborowski was a showman. He built four colossal aeroplane-engined cars in the 1920s which filled the crowds that saw – and heard – them at Brooklands with awe. They were as much as 27 litres in size, and he took one for a mad dash across the Sahara Desert with his wife. They were called 'Chitty Chitty Bang Bangs'; as they rarely revved above 1500rpm, you can understand why.

One man they left an indelible impression on was James Bond creator Ian Fleming, who wrote a 1964 children's book based on the story of a large vintage car with magical powers. Cubby Broccoli, producer of the 007 movies, turned Fleming's fairytale into a film with Roald Dahl's help.

ALBERT R. BROCCOLI presents
DICK VAN DYKE · SALLY ANN HOWES
LIONEL JEFFRIES
in IAN FLEMING'S
"CHITTY CHITTY BANG BANG" U
Producer ALBERT R. BROCCOLI Director KEN HUGHES
Filmed in SUPER-PANAVISION®
TECHNICOLOR® UNITED ARTISTS

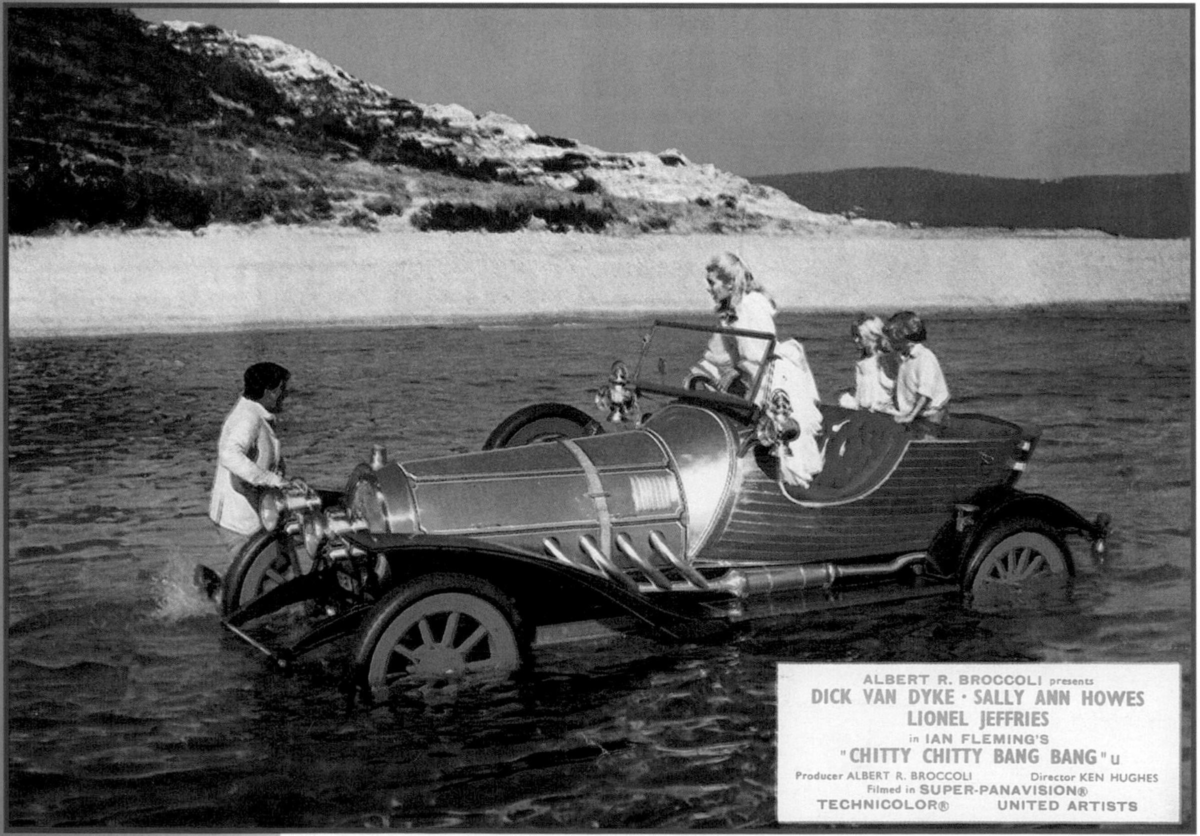

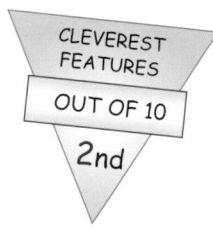

CLEVEREST FEATURES OUT OF 10
2nd

Dick Van Dyke and Sally Ann Howes take to the water in Chitty Chitty Bang Bang, proving its magical seaborne powers did work (as long as its axles didn't go any deeper, that is).

No childhood of the late 1960s was complete without seeing it through a frenzy of Kia-Ora and popcorn.

The cinematic Chitty Chitty Bang Bang was no aero-engined leviathan, however, but was specially built by Alan Mann Racing. It had a V6 Ford 3-litre engine and automatic transmission – although the sounds of a veteran Hispano

MAD for it! Who could resist the magical star of one of the best children's films of all time? Its owner, who exhibits the car around the country, has vowed never to sell it – even refusing a $10.9m offer from Michael Jackson in 1991 – and now a visually similar Chitty is delighting the crowds on the London stage in an acclaimed new CCBB musical.

On the *Chitty Chitty Bang Bang* set at Pinewood Studios in 1968; note the second mock-up of the car, with a helpful reminder of what the windscreen was made of to avoid those untoward thespian nosebleeds.

Suiza were dubbed on to the film for 'authenticity'. Special effects man Rowland Whett saw to it that Chitty appeared to fly and swim, as lovable inventor Caractacus Potts – played by Dick Van Dyke – intended.

Broccoli kept the car at Pinewood Studios but, when no sequel seemed likely, he sold it to professional clown Pierre Picton in 1972, complete with GEN 11 number plate, with a proviso that Broccoli had first refusal if he got sick of it.

 SAD for it! Vintage car grumblers have always maintained that the filmic star car bears very little resemblance to Zborowski's incredible creations, and some cynics have even suggested that Chitty can't actually fly or cope with anything deeper than a small puddle. . . .

This is the car Michael Jackson just couldn't buy, complete with its useful wings for those impromptu take-offs. No aeroplane engine under that long bonnet, just a Ford Zephyr V6 motor.

There is little doubt that many drivers would claim to require nothing more from a car than four wheels, an engine, a steering wheel and some brakes. In some cases, they might even insist on a little bit of rudimentary weather protection. With these simple elements, they would be perfectly happy to go about their driving business for evermore.

Indeed, you might be surprised to learn that it was a combination of the basics like this that formed the

February 1967 and Russian newsagency TASS issues this picture of the brand-new Zaporozhets ZAZ 966, a rather unappetising rear-engined economy model for those who weren't 'fortunate' enough to be able to afford a Moskvich.

MOST ATTRACTIVE OUT OF 10 9th

The dying days of a legend saw the Mini, always invigorating to drive but intentionally stark in concept, swept upmarket. You *could* get the plain version (in the background) but you were encouraged to invest in a fancified Cooper with lots of fripperies (foreground).

inspiration for the original 1959 Mini. Its creator Sir Alec Issigonis was an austere sort of a chap: he liked a cigarette, so an ashtray was part of the Mini's package. But he hated listening to the radio when he drove, so there was none. Instead of interior handles, there was a primitive cord with which to slam the doors shut, and the dashboard, such as it was, consisted of a single speedo in the centre of a shelf that ran across the front of the passenger cabin.

By the time the car ceased production, over four decades later, it was still possible to buy a new Mini that had the minimum

of frippery; however, most buyers of what was by now something of a living antique, loaded their new Minis up with flashy extras, everything from a walnut-and-leather interior to a bank of four spotlights on the car's stubby nose. Issigonis, no doubt, was spinning in his grave with indignation, but it was a clear indication that, in fact, few drivers enjoy their motoring devoid of luxuries and gadgets.

You're unlikely to see many Volgas in the west, particularly one as old as this 1965 M-21K model, so you'll have to put up with the fuzzy but original 1960s colour picture. The rugged beast has long been Russia's staple taxi.

In the age before motorways were built people were happy to trundle around Britain in stark motors like the Ford 100E Squire you see here. Which is just as well, as even a few miles on the M1 or M6 in this mid-1950s buzzbox was enough to make a motorbike-and-sidecar seem luxurious.

In many countries, however, deluxe motoring has never been an option. We are all familiar with the rough and ready nature of Russian cars, such as the notoriously downmarket Lada. Its larger and smaller siblings are, perhaps, less familiar to Western eyes but are just as uncompromising when it comes to creature comforts. Russian cars have always been built with toughness in mind, and the Volga saloon, first introduced in 1955 and still in production today, was intended for a life of service as the country's principal taxi. Volgas have always been robust and roomy but, in comparison with even the most basic of Ford Granada or Vauxhall Carlton in Britain, they are slow, crude and jarring.

The Lada's little brother, the Zaporozhets, came along in 1960. Initially a poorly executed copy of the Fiat 600, this awful little car was what you could aspire to if there was no chance of you ever being able to afford a Lada – much less a Moskvich. A handful

were sold in Benelux countries during the 1960s under the brand name of Yalta, but Belgium and the Netherlands were as far as they penetrated the sophisticated European market. Today you can still buy a Zaporozhets, albeit now a small and fairly conventional family hatchback. Tellingly, however, they are still so

The plastic-bodied Carmel – this is a 1966 model – and its Sussita and Sabra siblings are still the only indigenous Israeli cars. Designed by Reliant, they relied on imported Ford parts and a clientele motivated by patriotism rather than good consumer sense.

shoddy that their sales continue to be confined to within Russian borders.

The everyday basic cars our dads can probably recall from the 1950s were often little more than delivery vans with windows punched out of their metal sides and a small and usually pretty uncomfortable seat positioned where normally there would be tins of paint or trays of cakes. In this way the Commer Cob begat the Hillman Husky and the Ford Thames sired the Ford Squire,

From its sliding windows to its crude exterior door hinges, the Reliant Fox had corners cut aplenty, but it didn't stop Tandy Industries of the Isle of Wight from using this little workhorse as a basis for a pint-sized motorhome.

dismal and utilitarian vehicles all of them. In those pre-Mini days of the mid-1950s the no-frills alternative to such motoring fare was provided by a flotilla of three-wheeled devices, the best and most competent of which was, of

The Chinese models are no accident: Mercedes-Benz was angling for a lucrative contract to put China on wheels in the mid-1990s with this design prototype and a whole range of alternatives. And basic it would indeed have needed to be to be affordable nationwide.

course, made by Reliant. This Tamworth, Staffordshire enterprise also developed a thriving sideline in exporting the bare essentials for fledgling motor industries in unlikely countries.

Reliant embarked on this scheme in 1958 when it helped to establish car-making in Israel for the very first time. The Sussita, an ugly and unprepossessing little estate car, consisted of mostly Ford-related mechanical elements fitted to a simple chassis and clothed with an amateurish glassfibre body. Reliant supplied the oily bits and packed them off to the Middle East, while Haifa-based Autocars Ltd produced the bodywork itself and assembled the vehicles into something like customer-ready form. As an 'instant' motor industry, it was about as simple to

The unlovely Tata was, at least, an all-Indian design. This is a Loadbeta 2.0D van but, despite appearances, it's not an off-roader: the high ground clearance is for potholed roads from Delhi to Bombay, not wet grass at Sussex gymkhanas, so selling these bone-shakers in the UK has been hard work.

CLEVEREST FEATURES OUT OF 10 3rd

Chrysler tried to re-invent the Citroën 2CV with its Composite Concept Vehicle, a back-to-basics four-door family car for poor countries that was claimed to be as easy as a toy to assemble.

Reliant engine, that was so primitive it did not even possess wind-up windows. Reliant, however, optimistic as usual, even decided to sell it to the British, flagging it as a versatile workhorse that could be used for just about any task. Predictably, maybe, it was a flop.

There always used to be this theory that Third World nations would be completely happy with third-rate products. The natives in poverty-stricken countries were always assumed to desire only the most simplistic of road transport. In 1972, for example, General Motors schemed a small 'General Purpose' vehicle that, it said, was ideal for the back of beyond. Its simple construction could be achieved by, according to GM, just about any old peasants, provided they were prepared to spend their precious foreign currency

prepare as a Pot Noodle. And about as appetising to the average, car-hungry Jerusalem motorist. Later make-do-and-mend models in this vein included the Sabra sports car and the Carmel family saloon. But by the mid-1980s these cobbled-together cars were proving just too basic, even as battered runabouts on out-of-the-way kibbutzes.

Reliant helped to establish similar ventures in Turkey, and also Greece, where a factory built some bizarre three-wheeled delivery vans from kits of parts imported from our own West Midlands. The Greek firm was called Mebea, and in the 1980s it also assembled the Fox. This was a small pick-up, with four wheels and a

Maybe the pith helmet betrays what General Motors really thought about 'emerging' nations in 1972, as it tried to tempt them to build these ultra-simple trucks at home while being obliged to buy kits of Vauxhall-made parts to power them.

UGLIEST CAR

OUT OF 10

10th

SY · LC 76

on buying kits of Vauxhall-made components to ensure that the resulting little trucks could actually move. Mortifyingly, the small businessmen in places like Chad or Thailand elected instead to buy a perfectly civilised Toyota pick-up – or even something coarse but homegrown, like India's Tata vehicles.

Similarly, giant car-making corporations such as DaimlerChrysler have consistently revealed design studies for cars it feels would be ideal for the automotive underprivileged, ranging from a series of vehicles intended for China's burgeoning car-owning public, to a latterday Citroën 2CV, the Chrysler

Obviously I don't want to make a song and dance about it, but if a policeman saw six groovers behaving like this on the move in a VW 181 there'd definitely be 'words'. Volkswagen's stripped-down field car was sold as 'The Thing' in the US.

CCV. This stands for Composite Concept Vehicle, and it was a plastic family car which, claimed its makers, could easily achieve 50mpg, was totally recyclable, and was as easy to assemble as a toy. But you can't get away from the idea that, just as we like the Fiat Punto and Volkswagen Polo here in Western Europe, these are the kinds of car our impoverished cousins in less prosperous places would also relish.

On the other hand, when Volkswagen itself decided to create a stripped-down version of the Beetle in 1969, it found that trying to interest military customers in the 181 was well-nigh impossible. So the open-topped, armoured-looking machine was foisted upon the Americans, possibly with a view to breaking into the beatnik market. Volkswagen chose not even to confront the tricky subject of customer perception: it marketed the 181 as The Thing!

Renault had an adventurous spirit too, when the French company decided to re-invent the basic car in a stylish new package as the 1992 Twingo. This brilliant little car, however, was deemed just too radical for a Britain thought to be in love with shag-pile carpets and twinkly trinkets, and the car has always been denied us.

MOST ATTRACTIVE
OUT OF 10
6th

The friendly face of the 1992 Renault Twingo proved a cheap economy car need not reflect either of those values, and yet the French company decided it was too radical for us Brits and steadfastly refused to import it. Which was a crying shame.

Built: 1975 in Paris,
France
Engine: four-cylinder,
1129cc
Top speed: unknown
Sold in the UK? No
Number made: 1

COUNTRY MEETS TOWN IN A DOLLED-UP CLASSIC

It's a simple beast, the Citroën 2CV, its two cylinders clattering and its curvaceous body leaning wildly on even the widest of bends. Low on acceleration and even meaner on petrol. But it could never be called modern. It had been introduced in 1948 as no-frills rural transport for French farmers' wives and, while enduringly trusty, it belongs to another, slower age. On safety alone, it's

MAD for it! With the Volkswagen Beetle and Mini rejuvenated for a fresh generation, everyone now loves these modern 'classics' And Citroën was there decades before them with what would surely have been a fun and characterful little urban runabout.

DAFTEST FEATURES

OUT OF 10

1st

The 2CV had an amazingly long life, manufactured in an ancient factory in the centre of Paris before being pensioned off to Portugal for its final few years.

Seems like a funny way to extend the 2CV's life, adding twiddly hood irons, a vintage-style grille and fancy wheels. At least the four-cylinder engine, from the Citroën GS, gave it some much-needed poke.

To keep the 2CV going way past its true sell-by fate, Citroën issued numerous special editions, including this stripey little numero called the Beachcomber.

right down there with combine harvester blades and two-bar electric fires on bathroom floors.

Which all makes this bizarre 1975 confection even more amazing: the Metro was an attempt to fly in the face of modern cars like the VW Golf and Alfasud and keep the 2CV alive for even longer.

This gentrified prototype, with its chintzy fake hood irons, chrome grille and fancy wheels, came with twice the punch of the usual, snail-like 2CV – under its bonnet was the flat-four cylinder Citroën GS engine.

Thankfully good sense prevailed and Citroën let the humble 2CV live out its days – which ended some thirteen years later, soon after production had been transferred from central Paris to Portugal – without the hot-rod treatment, while developing proper modern cars like the Visa and BX.

A very early production example of the 2CV from 1949; the car was designed for farmers who wanted cheap transport that could be relied upon not to damage eggs on the way to market.

 SAD for it! One of the 2CV's original aims was that it could be driven across a ploughed field loaded with eggs, and none should so much as crack. Big engines and chrome fittings were for other cars. . . .

It might have had a sunroof and a bonnet shaped like a tin snail, but even these advantages did not outweigh the fear of being involved in an accident in one. . . .

THE DAIHATSU TREK IN DETAIL

Built: 1985 in Osaka, Ikeda, Japan
Engine: two-cylinder, 617cc
Top speed: unknown
Sold in the UK? No
Number made: 1

DAFTEST FEATURES

OUT OF 10

3rd

THE ONE-SEATER, OFF-ROAD, MOTORISED TENT TYPE-THING

It might be etched on your mind that Japanese car makers got where they are by copying what Europe and America already did so successfully. But you can hardly accuse them of being mere mimics today. Every couple of years the Tokyo motor show throws up more wacky ideas and quirky design concepts than you'd find at a dozen British motor shows. Funnily enough, Daihatsu, one of Japan's smaller makers and controlled by the giant Toyota, begets more than its fair share of 'concept' cars.

Here's one from 1985 when Daihatsu presented an amazing thirty-two concept cars in Tokyo under the 'Small

The 1985 Daihatsu Trek, ideal for those carefree trips into the wild, as long as you don't mind going on your own.

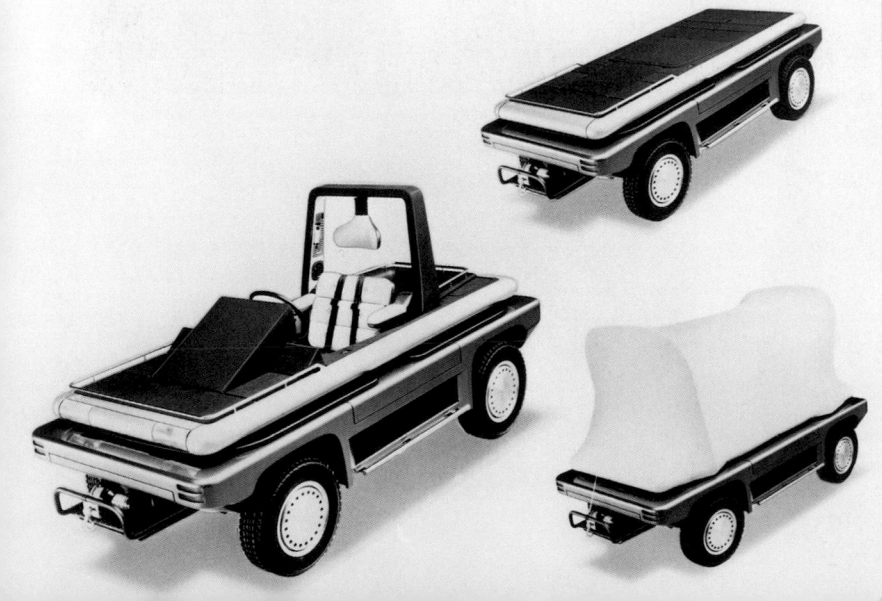

 MAD for it! What could be more fun than setting off into the wild at the helm of a Trek? And what better motorised friend to have if you need somewhere to rest that weary head, plus some canvas just in case a night under the stars turns wet and windy?

Fold the seat down and the Trek became a bed; put the top up and it was a handy motorised tent that would keep the dew – and mosquitoes – at bay.

Vehicles With A Big Dream' banner. It was designed specifically to turn the average ten-year old quadbike addict back into a boy scout.

The Trek, with its single seat, rugged construction and high ground clearance, would certainly have been a lot of fun off road. However, should junior have found himself too far away from home at night to get home, the steering column could be dropped away out of sight, the seat could be folded shut, and the Trek could became a comfy single bed.

Mosquitoes or downpours? No problem: simply pop the instant tent up for a perfect night's sleep.

The Trek never went into production, of course. Not very surprising, really.

▲ This vehicle is the 1989 Daihatsu Hijet Dumbo, another daft-looking idea for minimal motoring from the fertile collective mind of the company's experimental department.

SAD for it! Car designers, you would have thought, are busy people – far too busy to waste their time on things like this. They claimed the Trek was supposed to signify a 'spirit of adventure', but it probably did more damage to Daihatsu's flimsy 1980s credibility than good.

And here we have the Daihatsu Mira Milano, a somewhat brazen attempt to put a bit of curvaceousness back into car design – like the Trek, it was another instant relic. ▶

THE DAIMLER SILVER
FLASH IN DETAIL

Built: 1953 in Coventry,
West Midlands and
Acton, London
Engine: six-cylinder,
2952cc
Top speed: unknown
Sold in the UK? No
Number made: 1

DOCKERS' DREAM DAIMLER WAS A REAL FLASH IN THE PAN

Sir Bernard and Lady Norah Docker were the self-styled King and Queen of Daimler in the 1950s. Although he was the parent company BSA's boss, it was the influence and cash of his railway rolling stock mogul father that propelled him to the top. She grew up above a Derby butcher's shop but managed to be widowed by two millionaires by the time she wed Sir Bernard.

Each year at the motor show from 1950 to '55, the Dockers ensured Daimler was the centre of tabloid attention with a show-stopping special car – 'concept cars' as we know them today.

The first had gold-plated fittings, 1952's car lizardskin seats and double-glazing, while a body covered with tiny, hand-painted

The Daimler Silver Flash, built in 1953 by Hooper to Lady Norah Docker's personal tastes, provided some much-needed glamour at the Earl's Court motor show.

MAD for it!

There wasn't an awful lot to get excited about in early 1950s Britain, and Bernard and Norah's annual Daimler extravagance was something to look forward to. The cars never made it to production, but usually boasted a feature or two that were ahead of their time.

The 1952 Daimler 3-litre Regency, on which the Silver Flash was based. This is not a great lumbering 1950s saloon but, said Daimler, a 'beautifully proportioned six-seater'. Hmm. . . .

stars graced 1954's effort, and 1955 saw the 'Golden Zebra', for which unfortunate eponymous animals were slain to produce its interior trim.

These Docker pet projects got publicity but were so enormously costly to make – at BSA's London coachbuilder Hooper – that Sir Bernard was eventually booted off the Daimler board for his excessive spending, taking his pushy wife away with him.

'Silver Flash' was the 1953 show car, pictured here. Smaller than the other models in the series (it was based on the Daimler Regency model), it was just as opulent, with solid-silver hairbrushes and propelling pencils built into the interior, and fitted red crocodile skin luggage.

It did, though, make a stab at being advanced, with its lightweight aluminium body, aerodynamic front and tinted glass sunroof. The car was last seen at an American auction but, like all the 'Docker Daimlers', is no doubt in the ownership of a loving enthusiast.

 Coachbuilder Hooper was more accustomed to turning out formal but elegant cars. This Daimler 3-litre Regency has Hooper's famous razor-edged 'Empress' bodywork.

SAD for it!

Fiddling while Rome burns: Daimler, Britain's oldest carmaker, was in serious decline by 1953, thanks to Docker's inept stewardship. Indulgent projects like the Silver Flash only hastened its demise, a drift eventually arrested by Jaguar's acquisition of Daimler in 1960, and the marque's relegation to the position of 'Posh Jag'.

Other firms thought they could have a go at turning the Regency into a sleek coupé too; this one was made by Switzerland's Ghia-Aiglo for the 1955 Geneva Motor Show.

Built: 1977 in Maldon, Essex
Engine: electric motor
Top speed: 30mph
Sold in the UK? No
Number made: 1

A PLUG-IN PRAM THAT FAILED TO MAKE 1970s BRITAIN BUZZ

One hundred and eight: the production record for any British electric car. But, even then, it hardly represents real 'sales': the vast majority of the Enfield 8000 electric cars made in around 1976 were ordered by regional electricity boards for evaluation.

One group of Essex entrepreneurs, however, got closer than most to putting Britain on the battery-powered map. Electraction, led by an ex-Ford designer called Roy Haynes, bombarded motor shows in London and Chicago with designs for a two-door saloon, a two-seater roadster, a van and a

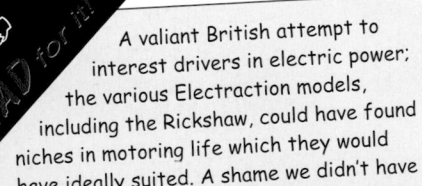
The fringed 'Surrey' top and the striped seats hint at the Electraction Rickshaw's intended use in life – pottering soundlessly around holiday resorts.

MAD for it! A valiant British attempt to interest drivers in electric power; the various Electraction models, including the Rickshaw, could have found niches in motoring life which they would have ideally suited. A shame we didn't have a little more faith in electric cars in that 'Ford Capri' decade.

July 1986 and all that remains of the Rickshaw's electric dreams is this sorry-looking mess, apparently abandoned behind a shed in Thames Ditton, Surrey.

pick-up featuring packs of heavy-duty Oldham lead acid batteries and a 7.5bhp electric motor.

The strange Rickshaw was the fifth variant. Like the others, it used a mixture of Vauxhall parts and glassfibre, but it was aimed at sun-drenched holiday resorts or similar 'contained environments' where its 55-mile range and 30mph top speed would be ideal.

And if the beat of the sun's rays became too intense, the fringed 'Surrey' top at the back could be raised as a handy automotive parasol.

'Electraction's marketing director', said the company in 1977, 'has the job of holding back the avalanche of potential customers until production gets underway.' Alas, despite relentless promotion, support from the British Trade Development Office, and a merger with famous sports car firm AC, Electraction seems never to have sold any vehicles – like so many

A simple light commercial vehicle version of the Rickshaw surely could have been popular, even if only on station concourses or, dare I venture, milk rounds.

other British electric car hopefuls, dashed by the market's total indifference to plug-in motoring.

The prototype Rickshaw ended up head-first in an overgrown ditch in Thames Ditton, Surrey, from where it was rescued by a local collector.

SAD for it! Electric cars, then as now, have severe limitations – a range of just 55 miles being the most obvious. The electricity still has to be generated somewhere, causing pollution or environmental damage. Electraction wasn't ahead of its time – there probably never will be an electric car era.

This is the Electraction EVR-1, the most 'normal' of Electraction's prototypes – and, yes, the front end and doors are pirated from an unsuspecting Vauxhall Chevette.

MAD COPY-CARS

In 1946, with the Second World War finished, US shipbuilder Kaiser decided it would enter the car business. It certainly had the resources like plant (Ford's old Willow Run factory, which had built B-24 Liberator bombers) and steel to get on with the job, but to design the cars it hired a freelance product designer called Howard Darrin to come up with something to get the customers interested – and away from their Buicks and Chevrolets.

The 1946 prototype was technically interesting with its front-wheel drive and unitary construction (neither of which would make it to the showroom) but its most striking feature was its styling. Any suggestions of 'mudguards', separate wings, free-standing bonnet or any other carriage throwbacks were banished. This was full-width, 'pontoon' styling at its most brutal – some hated it, thinking it slab-sided and ugly. The punters

UGLIEST CAR

OUT OF 10

4th

The uncompromisingly slab-sided Kaiser Frazer sedan, from the pen of Howard Darrin, was introduced in 1947 to rapturous acclaim from buyers, and instantly set a trend for 'full-width' styling that made most of its contemporaries appear redundant overnight.

And here is the 1951 Ford Consul, Britain's answer to the demand for an up-to-the-minute looking motor car like the Kaiser; the sister Zephyr and Zodiac models shared the same body style but with a bigger engine, a more prominent grille and various upmarket trimmings.

The Fiat 1400 and 1900 family saloons – this is a 1900, being discussed over drinks by a group of Italian style critics (I like to think, anyway) – was one of many cars that brought the modern Kaiser look to Europe, albeit on a much smaller scale.

certainly liked them – 140,000 were sold in 1947 – but the car was significant in another way: that distinctive, straight through 'fender-line' became one of the most influential features in automotive history. Pretty much every saloon car that made its debut between 1949 and 1955 adopted the Kaiser 'look', including Ford in Britain, whose Consul/Zephyr took it up, and Fiat, whose similarly sized 1400/1900 models did the same. As did the Borgward Hansa, Singer SM1500, Alfa Romeo 1900 and Standard Vanguard. The Kaiser is one of the most copied cars in history.

Many subsequent car copies, however, have been far more straight-forward: the motoring equivalent of the

Vintage Bentleys have long been worth a king's ransom, quite apart from their impracticality in everyday use. However, twenty or more years ago rusty, post-war Bentley Mk6/R-type saloons were plentiful and unwanted, serving as the perfect basis for some characterful and none-too-faithful replicas from Mallalieu.

UGLIEST CAR
OUT OF 10
9th

This neo-classic horror is called the Valiente and hails from 1981. Its vague inspiration could be any number of great American roadsters of the 1930s but the sad fact is that the middle bit is nothing more exciting than a Triumph Spitfire. And with a bonnet that long, any owner surely had to have an adequacy problem. . . .

tribute band, the 'replicar', has been around for decades, probably starting with the Excalibur in 1964. The recipe is a simple one: take a car design that everyone adores but no-one can own because it's too rare and valuable to get their hands on – as well as being, quite possibly, far too temperamental for modern motoring life – and recreate it using plentiful mechanical parts and a large dollop of imagination.

In the early 1980s, for example, a British company called Mallalieu tapped into the demand for vintage Bentleys by buying rotten R-type saloons of the post-war era, stripping their rusty bodies off and building on the remaining chassis a variety of pseudo vintage machines which were fun and easy to use, and almost looked like the real thing.

In Brazil at around the same time, a furniture company called MP helped slake the thirst for classic English sports cars like the MG TD with a plastic lookalike, except running on recycled Volkswagen Beetle parts. One of them was even used by Roger Moore in the 007 film *Moonraker*.

Contemporary replica makers in the USA, like Valiente, actually used the ready-made centre section from a Triumph Spitfire for its 1980s-made roadster, a V8-powered vintage pastiche

intended to rekindle the lost glamour of 1930s Hollywood. Look closely at the picture and you'll see the Triumph bit right there in the middle. And in the late 1960s Italian company Siata put together its idea of a Latin Morgan or MG on the basis of brand new Fiat 850s.

As a 'vintage' car, it fooled no-one, but had a sort of lissom charm to it – and also popped up as the star car in the cult French film *Traffic*.

But when is a copy a rip-off? Well, today Morgan has the classic profile of its timeless two-seater registered as a

On a hazy day it could almost have been a genuine MG TD coming at you through the Brazilian woods, but then you would hear the Volkswagen engine and see the ersatz detailing, and probably know it was an MP Lafer. This is a 1978 example; the car was also driven by James Bond, believe it or not.

Not quite sure what the 1967 Siata Spring roadster was supposed to emulate, but there are traces of all sorts of classic sports cars in there, from MGs to Alfa Romeos. What I do know is that the engine came from Fiat and the car was a big star of the Jacques Tati film *Traffic*.

The De Tomaso Deauville, unveiled in 1972, had an uncanny resemblance to a certain luxury car made in Coventry and boasting a feline name. Under those svelte lines, however, the power comes from an American Ford V8, while the interior shatters any illusion that this is a Jaguar XJ6.

trademark, so woe betide anyone who thinks he can set up shop making fake Plus 8s. Alessandro de Tomaso did not appear to have any such qualms when he launched the De Tomaso Deauville in 1974, a Ford-engined luxury car that, to the casual observer, was the spit of the Jaguar XJ6. Had the Italian model really posed a threat to Coventry's supremacy in the field then they might have taken the matter further, but the Deauville proved to be very small beer indeed, and only a few hundred were sold. That was not the case with the Honda N360/600, launched in 1966, though: you really did need to look twice to be sure it wasn't a Mini. Once you heard it, you would be in doubt because the car had an air-cooled twin-cylinder engine although, like the Mini, it also had front-wheel drive. And anyway, Honda soon left the car behind, and in fact presaged cars like the Metro when it launched the phenomenally successful Civic hatchback in 1972.

Imitation as the sincerest form of flattery, or necessity as the mother of invention? Either idiom will do for the first Land Rover. Developed on a farm in Anglesey in 1947, it wasn't just a bit like a war-time Jeep turned into a farmer's friend – the prototype was actually based on old Jeep parts. One clue was the wheelbase, identical on both. The production Land Rover, of course, was very much its own design when it was launched in 1948, but the inspiration was always obvious.

Maybe when you copy what you've done already, it's not such a rip-off. The Spanish Pegaso truck company, for instance, built a small number of fast and exciting V8 sports cars in the 1950s, and revived the design in 1991 for a pain-staking replica (albeit one powered by a British Rover V8 engine and, indeed, the whole car was built in the UK) to celebrate the company's tradition of

If casually glimpsed as it buzzed past you, you might easily have mistaken this Honda N600 for a Mini. True, they were both front-wheel drive, but the Honda had a twin-cylinder 600cc engine with air-cooling, and was no doubt far better built.

The rather lovely 1991 Z-103 undergoes some shakedown testing in the UK: the car was built to celebrate the engineering traditions of Spanish company Pegaso – yet with a Rover V8 engine – but only a dozen were made before the enterprise was abandoned.

No sooner had the Second World War ended than Willys announced its 'civilian' version of the Jeep. It was called the CJ-2A, and its totally practical concept was virtually unchanged from the vehicle that had helped to liberate Europe – no-one had ever consciously 'designed' the way it looked at all.

Here is one of the very earliest Land Rover prototypes, being demonstrated in the most agricultural role possible and featuring a single, central driving seat (changed on production models). The Land Rover was closely based on Jeep parts, even possessing an identical wheelbase at this stage.

engineering excellence. Only around a dozen were made.

But few copies are as lovingly accurate as the Canadian-made Timmis. Since 1968 this tiny firm has been creating exact replicas of the classic 1934 Ford V8 Model 40 roadster. Each car takes a year to complete because many of its parts have to be hunted down from scrap 1940s Ford V8-engined cars. The other bits are specially made copies of original features, even though the outwardly identical body of the Timmis is plastic in place of the venerable Ford's original steel. . . .

MOST ATTRACTIVE
OUT OF 10
10th

MOST SURPRISING
OUT OF 10
7th

There is very little to distinguish this from a real Ford V8 Model 40 from around 1934. In fact, it is a Timmis, a Canadian-built replica that is so faithful some parts are probably interchangeable. It's been around for thirty-four years and each one takes a year to build.

Built: 1992 in Paris, France
Engine: four-cylinder, 1584cc
Top speed: unknown
Sold in the UK? No
Number made: 2

INVENTED BY A DIAMOND GEE-ZEUR TO SAVE THE PEDESTRIAN

You had to admire Philippe Charbonneaux, aged 75 and a French industrial designer of some standing, because, to many, his Ellipsis was the laughing stock of the Paris motor show in 1992. Yet the thinking behind his diamond wheel-pattern runabout, with both front and rear steered wheels, was earnest enough.

Presumably just emerged from the chateau workshop of evergreen French designer M. Charbonneaux, the Ellipsis is ready to roll – watch out you other road users.

MAD for it! With an incredible design career to his credit, M. Charbonneaux was still trying to innovate when most of us would find pottering about in the garden rather tiring. Plus, the Ellipsis could be said to have taken a new and refreshing approach to passive safety, an issue sure to become important in years to come.

It could allegedly do a U-turn in a space barely twice its length, and its two steered wheels meant it could wiggle into tight Parisian parking spaces. Its long contours with a softly rounded 'point' at either end meant, claimed Charbonneaux, the car was much safer in accidents, deflecting pedestrians rather than ploughing into them, and 'sliding' away from most impacts.

Apparently there was a Volkswagen Beetle engine powering the two central wheels but Charbonneaux's theories were never independently

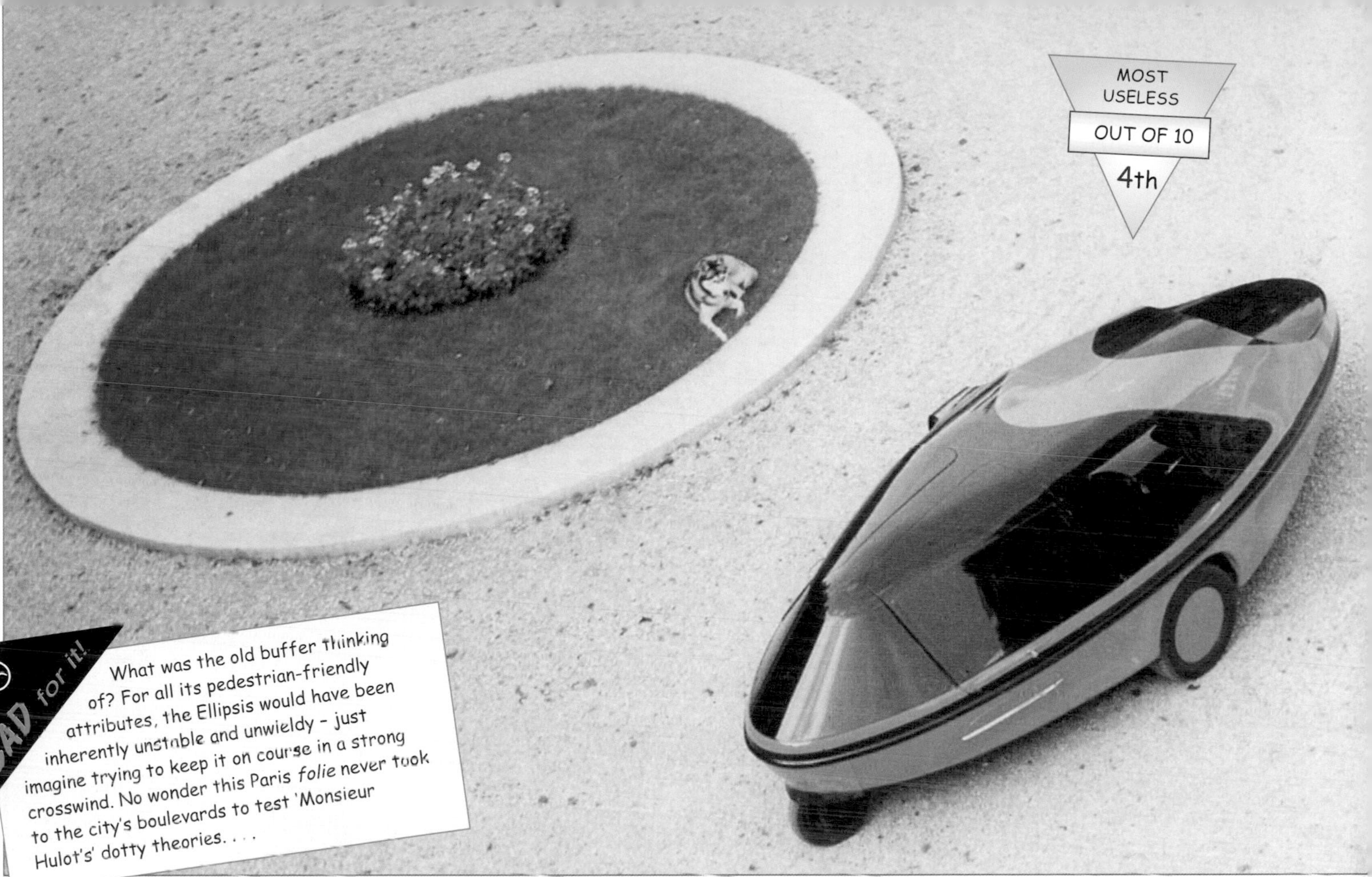

MOST USELESS
OUT OF 10
4th

SAD for it!

What was the old buffer thinking of? For all its pedestrian-friendly attributes, the Ellipsis would have been inherently unstable and unwieldy – just imagine trying to keep it on course in a strong crosswind. No wonder this Paris *folie* never took to the city's boulevards to test 'Monsieur Hulot's' dotty theories. . . .

'Soft' ends were supposed to be kinder to pedestrians and the diamond-pattern wheels, allegedly, meant the Ellipsis would have been a doddle to park on crowded streets.

tested. The whole car appeared to be nothing more than a thin plastic model – it was rolled breezily on to its show display by a workman, and the windows were conspicuously, and heavily, tinted, so it was impossible to see how on earth it actually worked.

Philippe Charbonneaux had had a hand in an American design classic: he was part of the team behind the Chevrolet Corvette sports car in 1953. He later designed the Renault 16, the ancestor of all today's five-door hatchbacks. Charbonneaux was still at it when he died aged 82 in 1999, a car design trouper to the end.

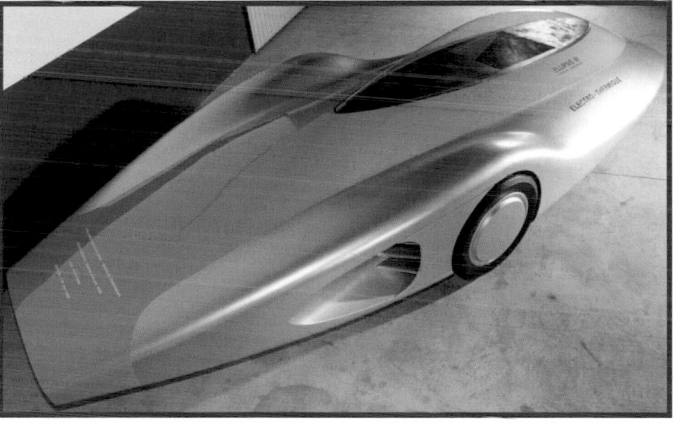

Even more far-fetched than the first Ellipsis, if you can imagine that, this later version used slippery aerodynamics to assist its electric powerplant.

Built: 1965 – now in
Milwaukee, Wisconsin,
USA
Engine: V8,
5360/5562/5000/7445cc
Top speed: 140mph
approx
Sold in the UK? No
Number made:
unknown

GRAND-DADDY OF REPLICARS IS A REFUGE FOR THE TASTE-CHALLENGED

In the USA industrial designers like Raymond Loewy, Walter Dorwin Teague and Norman Bel Geddes all tried their hands at car design, with varying success. Few were as influential, however, as Brooks Stevens. America's *Time* magazine called him 'The seer who made Milwaukee famous' and, in sixty-one years of industrial design, he had 550 clients and created thousands of pieces of work.

MAD for it!

If you like showing off, then an Excalibur is the car for you. Outrageous looks, exposed exhausts, a roaring V8 engine under that long, long bonnet, and masses of power on tap to make this stripped-down cruiser really shift. There are one or two in the UK: actor Tommy Steele was devoted to his.

'Nostalgic motoring with space-age dependability, performance and safety': the 'replicar' is born with the Excalibur, here shown in early two- and four-seater editions.

By 1979 the Excalibur's inspiration had shifted to 1930s Mercedes-Benz cars, and this SS Roadster was supposed to remind us – albeit vaguely – of its German sports car namesake.

Excalibur

In 1950 he single-handedly created the 'recreational' off-roader market with his Jeep Jeepster, a sort of four-wheel drive sports car, and along the way he drew the shapes of the Jeep Wagoneer, Volkswagen 411 and Studebaker Hawk.

His other legacy was inventing the 'replicar'. His first Excalibur roadster appeared in 1952 but he hit the jackpot in 1965 with the Excalibur SS, a *doppelganger* for the 1920s Mercedes-Benz SSK sports car but using a Studebaker chassis and V8 engine.

Just when you thought you'd seen it all, the four-seater Excalibur comes and hits you, metaphorically, between the eyes.

Two smoothies and their birds prepare for a run out in a mid-1980s Excalibur. We can assume none of them minded being stared at, especially the bloke in the white bow-tie.

A more recent Excalibur two-seater, ably demonstrating its oh-so-long bonnet – could there possibly be a bit of symbolism in there for its owners?

It was the first of a long series of 1920s and '30s-inspired cars, usually with Chevrolet power, that are still available today. In 1981 the styling was changed so the cars looked more like the flamboyant Mercedes-Benz 540K, and they mutated into a four-door saloon and even a stretch limo. However, Stevens' family-owned company went into receivership in 1986 and the venture was sold. They were always beautifully made, if in questionable taste. Still, it was a strange sideline for a man whose mission was usually modernity.

THE FORD COMUTA IN DETAIL

Built: 1967 in Dunton, Essex
Engine: electric motor
Top speed: 40mph
Sold in the UK? No
Number made: 6 approx

WHEN DAGENHAM DABBLED WITH ELECTRIC DREAMS

If you'd been ambling through South Kensington in 1972 you might have witnessed a rather poignant reminder of how the electric car dream has consistently failed to spark. It would have been the battery-powered Ford Comuta, scuttling quietly along en route from the Motor Show at Earl's Court to its final resting place – a quiet corner of the Science Museum.

Ford built several Comuta prototypes at its Research & Engineering Centre in Dunton, Essex in 1967. And they were certainly small: looking like Photo-Me booths on pedal car wheels, two Comutas measured the same length as one Cortina. It had to be this tiny, to avoid absolutely any superfluous weight, because its hefty cluster of lead-acid batteries meant the car actually weighed more than a Mini.

A Ford Cortina helps out to demonstrate just how small the Ford Comuta was; these two are part of a batch of experimental cars built by Ford in 1967.

Ford executives (from left to right) Laurie Maitland, Stanley Gillen, Leonard Crossland and Harley Copp examine the Comuta in 1967... and decide it will never sell.

 MAD for it! Every now and again you see a Ford-backed Th!nk electric car running around London – the first time that this clean and silent form of transport has caught on in the crowded capital. Which only proves the Comuta was along the right lines all those years ago.

RES 430E

Ford continued to think small: this is the Ghia-built Ford Trio of 1983, a 250cc three-seater that, at 98.4in long, was even shorter than the Comuta; it, too, never went on sale.

MOST USEFUL

OUT OF 10

3rd

The Th!nk city car project was recently bought by Ford, and the little electric runabouts are being seen around major cities some thirty-five years since Ford designed its own.

SAD for it! The Comuta looks as if it was made from old fridges and suitcases and its stubby and upright stance would have marked you out as an early electric car pioneer, had you been able to get your hands on one. Today's Th!nk is an improvement but there is a long way to go until the internal combustion engine is killed off by cars like these.

The Comuta was commendably silent and emissions-free. But for most urbanites, the Mini would also have run rings around Ford's baby electric car. Top speed was a power-sapping 40mph, with a mere 40-mile range if used very gingerly. Ford knew it was pointless proceeding with an electric car with such limited capabilities and, after this final journey, the Comuta was relegated to 'exhibit' status.

Interestingly, Ford returned to small electric cars with its purchase of the Norwegian Th!nk project and Richard Parry-Jones, one of its top design chiefs, has said he thinks 10 per cent of all new cars will be electric – but not until 2016! Still, Ford has just closed Th!nk down, so *it* won't be part of the revolution.

Built: 1963 in Detroit, Michigan, USA and Birmingham, West Midlands, UK
Engine: V8, 6384cc
Top speed: unknown
Sold in the UK? Yes
Number made: 1

AMERICAN HEARSE WAS A BRITISH UNDERTAKING

The noble British hearse isn't known for its speed. Most cover minimal and hallowed local mileage at such a gentle pace that they last for years. Wily undertakers throughout the land often keep their lustrous black vehicles in sedate service for decade after decade, and it's not unusual for loved ones to make their final journey in a vehicle even older than they were.

This 1963 vehicle was built by one of the country's most eminent hearse manufacturers, Thomas Startin Junior of Aston, Birmingham, at a time when the traditional Austin Princess base car was becoming obsolete and the later Daimler limo wasn't yet available: it started life as a Ford Galaxie 500.

DAFTEST FEATURES

OUT OF 10

4th

Probably the fastest hearse ever built in Britain, Thomas Startin's Galaxie 500, with its impressive but sombre lines, can in fact hardly ever have broken the speed limit.

Two Startin-bodied Austin A135 hearses head a line-up of brand-new funeral cars outside its works in Aston, Birmingham on a suitably gloomy day.

Nothing strange about that, you might think . . . until you remember that the Galaxie was one of the fastest cars then made in the US, and regularly thrashed such nimble sporting machines as Mini Coopers and Lotus Cortinas in saloon car racing in the hands of drivers like Jack Sears.

The racy 'ON 6' was bought by undertakers W.H. Scott and Son of Edgbaston, Birmingham in the early 1960s and was still used by the firm until about fifteen years ago, at which time it was scrapped and its useful parts stripped to keep another Galaxie going. A shame, that.

All we can assume is that, for the sadly departed enthusiast, it was once the only way to go.

The standard 1963 Ford Galaxie 500 seen here in extremely rare right-hand drive form. The car was a byword for style and luxury at a time when British rivals, by comparison, looked like they were ark-fresh.

MAD for it! With no suitable British limousines on which to work, Startin turned to one of America's most powerful, smooth and quiet cars as a basis for this well-designed conversion, creating a stylish and also dignified mode of transport for those final journeys. It's just a shame the car itself is now in that great scrapyard in the sky. . . .

SAD for it! This was never going to be a vehicle you'd be elated to see, and your average British mourner in the early 1960s was probably mildly horrified to see his Uncle Ernie about to meet his maker in the back of an American hearse. . . .

The Galaxie 500 in two-door coupé form; this 1963 example belongs to Goodwood owner Lord March, but similar cars were once a force to be reckoned with on Europe's race tracks.

MAD KIT CARS

Kit cars are the motoring equivalent of powdered egg or ersatz, acorn-based coffee – desperate products usually popular in desperate times. They have tended to flourish during Britain's periodic stretches of economic hardship, providing, reckon their designers, a glimmer of motoring pleasure when all around looks gloomy.

The first kit car era began in Britain in the very early 1950s, at a time when the country was still reeling from the after-effects of the Second World War. For many drivers the only motoring option available was a battered Austin Seven or Ford Popular, which could just about do its duty but was probably long past its best in the looks and general condition departments. However, a sporty-looking glassfibre body and a bit of mechanical nous could transform these unpromising objects into desirable little cars. Well, that was the theory anyway. . . .

The kit would invariably cost around £100, could be delivered by van, and would sometimes include a purpose-made chassis into which all the requisite metal organs could be transferred from the dilapidated donor vehicle. There were literally dozens to choose from, of which the Falcon range was among the

The Mini is a difficult car to improve on, most would agree, but Isle of Man-based Peel thought it could pull it off with its Viking kit, intended to transform a damaged or unloved Mini into a none-too-shabby coupé. But if you think it looks hideous from this view, you should see the front (on second thoughts, don't).

most popular. And the only thing standing between the purchaser and a nifty-looking finished sports car was his level of expertise at assembling and completing the whole caboodle, and the several long weekends needed to do so.

You can blame the Austin-Healey 'Frogeye' Sprite for spoiling the fun. It was launched in 1958, the year that Prime Minister Harold Macmillan told the

MOST WEDGE-SHAPED OUT OF 10 6th

The Nova could best be described as something of a council-house Lamborghini, possessing all the attention-grabbing looks of its Italian counterpart, yet relying almost totally on Volkswagen Beetle bits and pieces for motive power. For a time they were popular.

Models like this Falcon were among the best of the 1950s kit cars, designed to transform an unwanted Austin or Ford into a thing of beauty for the price of a week at Butlin's, and requiring only a set of spanners, a plentiful supply of Bovril, and some engineering determination.

A flattering view of the c. 1981 GP Talon, a sort of cross between Toyota MR2 and De Lorean, if you will, that could be knocked up on the drive for just a few quid, and could give hours of posing fun. Again, the Beetle generously donated its vital organs – your input was your time and the skin from your knuckles.

CLEVEREST FEATURES OUT OF 10 6th

MOST USEFUL OUT OF 10 4th

Perhaps the most famous British manufacturer of VW Beetle-based beach buggy kits is GP, and this example is the company's mid-1970s attempt at a commercial vehicle, called the LDV or Light Delivery Vehicle. Their very simplicity made them popular, as well as the promise of some Californian style in chilly old Blighty.

country that 'You've never had it so good'. At just £660, it was a modern and ready-built small sports car that rendered the kit cars obsolete literally overnight. The appearance of the Mini a year later, with its truly revolutionary design and very sporty handling, simply underlined how totally crummy the average kit car really was: amazingly,

within a few years the Mini itself was donating its vital organs to kit cars, such as the bizarre Peel Viking, a hideous-looking plastic coupé hailing from the Isle of Man in 1965.

But the kit car was not dead: it was set to rise again. In the mid-1970s, when British national morale had been brought to its knees by power cuts, strikes and

MOST
USELESS

OUT OF 10

1st

More Volkswagen-based mimicry: don't laugh, some people think this is a dead-ringer for the SS 100 Jaguar. The 1982 home-build Antique & Classic SS100, however, is all-Beetle beneath those copycat plastic panels. Depressingly, even the wire wheels are falsies.

the three-day week, the cash-strapped motorist was, once again, ready to embrace the home-build dream. By this time, obviously, the Austin Sevens and Ford Populars had all vanished, and many of the new breed of kits used the by-now ubiquitous Volkswagen Beetle as a basis because its rusty bodywork could be quickly and easily detached and jettisoned. You could, for instance, create your own Lamborghini in the front garden, using nothing more than a Nova kit, some spanners, some strong tea and a knackered Beetle. Or else a Californian-style beach buggy with the help of a kit of parts from GP and another unloved VW. The GP Talon of 1979 offered the chance of a homemade Fiat X1/9 with the added novelty of gullwing doors (this was a VW underneath too). Across the Atlantic there was a similar trend towards Beetle-based sports cars, many of which were replicas of classic designs that were, intrinsically, a travesty of the revered originals: how about, for example, a lookalike SS100 Jaguar with Wolfsburg power rattling away in the back?

UGLIEST
CAR

OUT OF 10

2nd

RICO

Wearing its glassfibre body around Ford Escort Mk II doors like an ill-fitting suit on a paunchy man, the Dutton Rico – this is a Series 2, so you can only imagine how awful the first incarnation looked – used the rest of the Escort's innards, plus some home-spannering to get it roadworthy.

The Hacker, from 1991, a kit car to turn an elderly Ford Fiesta into a nifty convertible looking uncannily like a newer Fiesta, was the work of Tim Dutton-Woolley. With prices of secondhand cars plummeting, however, can a car like this ever be popular again?

which utilised the good bits from unwanted Mk III Escorts.

Some other kits were more adventurous, such as the Norfolk-built Triking, a dead ringer for a Morgan three-wheeler of the early 1930s yet also boasting masses of power and excitement from a front-mounted Moto Guzzi V-twin motorbike engine. It came along in 1978 and is still available. And there was the short-lived Haldane, one of Scotland's few contributions to the car world, which was a pretty convincing copy of an Austin-Healey 3000, a costly

Back in the UK, the other main source of mechanical material for kit cars was Dagenham and its most famous resident, Ford. Literally thousands of Ford Escorts and Cortinas, some perfectly fit and healthy, gave up their lives to create Duttons, a bewildering range of sports and estate cars you could make at home simply by, metaphorically, adding hot water. There were plenty of alternatives, including the Fiesta-based Hacker and the Quantum,

Delighted Quantum owners pick up their cars from the factory in around 1993; as a better-than-average kit car at the time, it offered a stylish way to recycle an old Mk III Escort, and could be ordered as a kit of parts or fully assembled from the works. Today, though, wouldn't you prefer a secondhand MX-5?

MOST SURPRISING

OUT OF 10

8th

Not every kit car simply takes a care-worn banger and tarts it up. The Norfolk-built Triking is a beautifully made machine, using a new Moto Guzzi V-twin motorbike engine in a custom-made three-wheeled chassis/body to give vintage Morgan enjoyment without the aged drawbacks.

'Och, Mary, horsepower? That thing hasnae any' – hop in here and we'll go for a wee ride.' Yes, the Haldane was a Scottish kit car closely resembling an Austin-Healey 100/6 but which frugally used old Vauxhall parts to complete the illusion of classic car prosperity.

and desirable classic when the Haldane appeared in 1994, using an assortment of bits culled from moribund Vauxhalls.

In the new millennium, however, only two kit car makers have really survived and prospered. They are Caterham, which has manufactured versions of the Lotus Seven since 1973, and Westfield, which has flourished largely on the simple philosophy of making two-seater sports cars which are rather like Caterham Sevens. But occasionally both of these successful enterprises have done things that are a little bit mad. Caterham departed from its four-wheeled-motorbike roots to try its hand at a miniature TVR in the 1996 Caterham 21, while Westfield went left-field with its mid-engined XEi coupé in 1994. The 21 sold disappointingly despite its handsome looks, the XEi remained a prototype, and the kit car craze – in an environment where you can buy a secondhand Mazda MX-5 for peanuts – has gone into abeyance once more, and possibly for good.

Westfield has carved out a profitable niche for itself by making rapid, fine-handling sports cars to build yourself, in a very similar format to the established Caterham Seven. Forays away from this have tended to be fruitless, such as this mid-engined sports kit car, the XEi, from 1994.

THE FORD SAXON IN DETAIL

Built: 1963 in Dagenham, Essex
Engine: unknown
Top speed: unknown
Sold in the UK? No
Number made: 1

THE 'MISSING' CAPRI COULD HAVE BEEN THE PRIDE OF ESSEX MAN

The 1969 Ford Capri was billed as 'The car you always promised yourself' but the very first Capri or, more formally, the Ford Consul Capri, was a car customers vowed secretly not to buy. Slow, over-engineered and dripping with automotive Americanisms like fins, twin headlights and whitewall tyres, the 1961 Capri was a very lame attempt at a desirable 'personal' coupé. It was dropped after just three years. But Ford still tried to conjure up something dashing for the men of Essex. And this was it – Saxon, *circa* 1963.

Devoted car spotters will instantly recognise the 'CND' rear lights of the Mk I Cortina, from which Saxon was heavily derived. Even the scallop running from the nose to the neatly cut-off tail is Cortina-

 You can see the alternative side profile design through the glass of the Saxon's rear window; yet neither matched Ford's vision for an affordable and sporty two-door coupé.

The Ford Cortina from which the Saxon was derived: it was one of Britain's top sellers for twenty years – whose dad didn't lust after one?

like, although the hardtop is totally new. As with many pure 'styling exercises', Saxon is different on each side – you can just see the alternative side window treatment through the glass.

Saxon was widely deliberated from all angles by regiments of Ford's marketing brains. Their reaction, though, was a resounding thumbs-down, and it was another six years before the car that flash drivers longed for finally arrived.

One Cortina-based coupé that did hit the road was this one-off fastback Cortina GT, custom-built by leading design company Ogle for Stirling Moss's personal use.

MAD for it!

Natty styling for a two-seater coupé version of the Cortina – every dad's favourite during the 1960s – could have been a big hit with care-free, childless couples in the decade of the Rolling Stones, the mini skirt and, of course, the Campaign for Nuclear Disarmament.

SAD for it!

Ford missed the target badly when it tried its hand at a sporting car for the first time, and the Saxon was clearly a bit too closely related to the dreary old Cortina to fire up the marketing men. The success of the 1969 Capri proved this was a shrewd decision.

Ford finally hit the jackpot with the 1969 Capri – the wheel-spinning fantasy of every young blood at the time. This is a 1971 Capri 3000E, capable of 122mph to make it Ford's fastest-ever British production car at the time.

THE GATSO 'FLATTY' IN DETAIL

Built: 1949 in Heemsteede, Holland
Engine: six-cylinder, 1500cc
Top speed: unknown
Sold in the UK? No
Number made: 1

THE DUTCH SPEED FREAK WHO SLOWED EVERYONE ELSE DOWN

You can freely curse Maurice Gatsonides every time your car is flashed by a traffic enforcement camera. He was, after all, the Dutchman who invented the Gatso speed trap; he actually devised it as an electronic stopwatch for motor sport, to remove the human factor in measuring time and distance.

Maurice Gatsonides was fascinated by motor racing all his long life, and his mastery behind the wheel was poured into the design of this aerodynamic two-seater. His prowess in this and other cars later made him a Monte Carlo Rally champion, and he lived to a ripe old age.

MAD for it!

Mr and Mrs Gatsonides are re-united in 1991 with 'Flatty', his lightweight, Fiat-powered racing car that had wowed Dutch crowds in the 1940s.

For Gatsonides, who died four years ago aged 88, was passionate about and competitive in racing and rallying. He built and raced this strange-looking sports car in 1949 on an old Fiat chassis with a 1.5-litre six-cylinder engine. It caused a sensation at the Dutch Zandvoort track when it scattered MGs in its wake, and set a lap record for 1.5-litre cars of 63.7mph. The crowds loved it, nicknaming the waist-high two-seater 'Flatje', or Flatty.

Gatsonides was struggling to put his own V8-engined Gatso sports car, with a Perspex roof specially made by planemaker Fokker, into production but, in 1950, went bust and reluctantly sold Flatty to pay creditors.

A one-time KLM flight engineer, Gatsonides entered an old Hillman Minx in the Monte Carlo Rally in 1936, and went on to enter a further twenty-three times. His finest hour was winning in 1953 in Ford's works Zephyr Six.

The Flatty was eventually found abandoned in the 1970s and has now been restored by Dutch owner Joop Bruggeman; it's the only surviving Gatso car. Maurice is at the wheel here, with his wife Ciska.

CLEVEREST FEATURES

OUT OF 10

5th

In 1956 Maurice Gatsonides and co-driver Victor Gossington took this Standard Vanguard III to fourth in the Coronation Safari Rally, which was 2,700 miles long.

Monte Carlo Rally 1953 and Gatsonides' handily placed helpers chuck cold water over his Zephyr's red-hot brakes – helping him to a cool victory in the car.

SAD for it!

He might have enjoyed larking about on the track, but Gatsonides' legacy as the father of the speed camera has spelt misery for motorists since the early 1990s, helping to turn modern motoring from a cheering experience to a chore – especially if a Gatso snap leads to a hefty fine.

THE GKN FFF100 IN DETAIL

Built: 1973 in Coventry, West Midlands
Engine: V8, 7212cc
Top speed: 170mph
Sold in the UK? No
Number made: 1

EXCELLENT GOER, BRILLIANT STOPPER, PIRATED BY AUDI

Guest, Keen & Nettlefold Ferguson Formula Four-Wheel Drive 100 isn't quite so catchy, of course, but it does reveal a little more about this aggressive-looking beast. Built in 1973, the GKN FFF100 was claimed then to be the quickest ever car to accelerate from standstill to 100mph and then come to a halt again. At its first attempt, and on a wet test track, GKN engineers achieved this spine-tingling manoeuvre in 12.2sec – some 7sec better than the previous record, which had been undertaken on dry tarmac.

MAD for it!

Exciting British design and positively earth-shattering performance from this four-wheel drive road-rocket proved we could come up with the goods in the face of fierce competition from tough US 'muscle' cars and temperamental Italian exotica.

The ruggedly attractive hind quarters of the GKN FFF100, built expressly to show off the component maker's four-wheel drive and anti-lock braking hardware.

FFF 100

And of those 12.2 seconds, just 5.2 were spent stopping.

It was, effectively, a lightweight Jensen FF, having the same 426cu. in Chrysler Hemi engine and up-to-the-minute Ferguson four-wheel drive and anti-lock braking systems. The chunky styling, however, came from William Towns, the man behind the Aston Martin DBS.

Its massive speed and controllability were never offered to the public. GKN built just one FFF100 and that was solely as a rolling showcase for its own technology and materials. It appeared in a few motoring magazines but went largely unnoticed.

Except by Audi, that is. It knew a winner when it saw one and, seven years later, its turbocharged Quattro unleashed the concept virtually unchanged on the motoring world. It was a sensational, if predictable, success. Another one that got away from Britain. Ah, well. . . .

Little did we know that within seven years the performance package of the GKN FFF100 would be available to the driving public – thanks to those canny souls at Audi.

This is how stylist William Towns meant the FFF100 to look, and GKN got it mostly right – apart from the bonnet-top air intake, which was something of a crude mess on the actual car.

SAD for it!

No doubt about the acceleration and stopping capability but there's something a bit homespun about the styling – plus, of course, the Germans swooped in and nicked the plot for the Audi Quattro, leaving Britain with simply another passed-over innovator.

THE GENERAL MOTORS
FIREBIRD XP-21 IN
DETAIL

Built: 1954 in Detroit,
Michigan, USA
Engine: gas turbine
Top speed: unknown
Sold in the UK? No
Number made: 1

FABULOUS FIREBIRD POINTED TO A FUTURE THAT NEVER QUITE HAPPENED

You couldn't buy it, much less drive it on the road, but General Motors was determined to demonstrate it had seen the future – and that it worked. In the centre of the Arizona desert on a blisteringly hot 1954 day, test driver Mauri Rose gazes out through his plastic cockpit bubble as the Firebird jets towards the distance.

This was America's first gas turbine-powered car and, while its ultimate top speed was never recorded, it could develop 370bhp from compressed gas delivered to its rear wheels; its gasifier spun at a dazed 26,000rpm while its power unit gave 13,000rpm.

Styling was enough to make Dan Dare's jaw drop. The work of the legendary GM design chief Harley Earl, it was fashioned after the Douglas Skyray supersonic jet plane and made, like the then brand new Chevrolet Corvette, from glassfibre.

An alert-looking Mauri Rose gazes out of the plastic-covered cockpit of Firebird XP-21, America's first gas-turbine-powered car, in the middle of the desert in Phoenix, Arizona.

Mauri Rose (three times Indianapolis 500 winner, incidentally) again, this time piloting the delta-winged XP-21 along Daytona Beach in Florida in another test run in 1956.

Firebird XP-21 toured America as part of General Motors' 'Motorama' roadshow, an annual travelling circus of 'dream cars' in which it was, oddly, one of the few that actually functioned. Visitors in LA, Chicago, New York, Miami and San Francisco could scarce believe their eyes.

The GM dream sausage machine of the 1950s, however, relentlessly spewed out imaginary metal and, for 1955, there was lots of new stuff to ogle. But GM has always treasured XP-21, and today it's carefully stored at the company's research centre.

XP-21 was just the first of GM's fanciful 1950s dream cars: this is the Firebird III from 1958, electrically powered via a road-embedded magnetic strip and a joystick. Yeah, right. . . .

MAD for it!

A 'car' Gerry Anderson would be proud of but the incredible Firebird XP-21, complete with its jet-style power unit, really could take off – if not into the stratosphere then towards the horizon – at breakneck speed. So pity poor Mauri in his plastic bubble.

Well, at least one part of the Firebird XP-21 made it: the name. The Pontiac Firebird came along in 1967, General Motors' riposte to the Ford Mustang, and here its space-age namesake pays homage.

SAD for it!

Okay, so it could turn its wheels under its own steam (or, rather, gas) and it looked like a sci-fi fantasy, but the Firebird was a 'dream' car for those who never wake up. There has only been one gas turbine-engined production car, a Chrysler, but none was ever sold to the public.

There have been upwards of 6,500 car marques since Karl Benz fired up the first internal combustion engine in 1885. Clearly, not every one of them has survived. There are probably only around forty mainstream brands of car available today, and at least nine out of every ten new cars manufactured around the globe today are built by a mere ten giant corporations. In the car industry it really has been a case of survival of the fittest – and that tends to mean biggest.

Even some makes which are extremely well known have recently slipped into history. In the USA, General Motors recently decided to abandon the

MOST USELESS

OUT OF 10

6th

Lanchester had been one of the world's pioneering car companies, and its name still had a whiff of quality to it even in the early 1950s. Its parent company Daimler used the Lanchester brand on an all-new, unitary-construction car in 1956, but the Sprite was just too expensive to put into production and so, instead, it became Lanchester's swansong.

The last Plymouth Prowler, the sassy street-rod from Chrysler, was recently built and sold at auction for charity. It is the end of an era in more ways than one because corporate streamlining at DaimlerChrysler also means the Plymouth marque is destined for the dustbin of history too.

In many ways a very fine car, the Armstrong-Siddeley Star Sapphire of 1959 was destined to become the last of the line when two aircraft makers, Hawker Siddeley and Bristol, merged and found making cars was a sideline the new combine no longer wanted. Bristol Cars was luckier – it was sold off instead of being closed down.

Just five short years later it was a toss-up between Bristol and Armstrong-Siddeley after the merger of aeroplane rivals Bristol and Hawker Siddeley. Car-making was deemed to be peripheral, but what was to be done? The answer came swiftly and brutally: Bristol Cars was quickly sold to one of its dealers, and Armstrong-Siddeley – despite having an impressive new car just launched, the Star Sapphire – was simply closed down. A solid reputation

Oldsmobile name after exactly 100 years on sale; and rival Chrysler, now merged with Mercedes-Benz to form Daimler Chrysler, has also had a corporate clear-out. The Prowler, the two-seater hot rod that's been around for five years, is destined to be the last-ever Plymouth. Traditionalists might grumble, but in the world of big business there is little place for sentiment, it seems.

The killing-off of car marques has taken place routinely over the years. Okay, there wasn't an outcry in Parliament, but in 1956 Daimler decided that the historic Lanchester name was just not worth preserving. The company had designed a new Lanchester model, the Sprite, which boasted unitary con-struction, a 1.6-litre engine and a new type of automatic gearbox. However, when Daimler did its sums it realised this newcomer would be impossibly expensive to bring to the market.

Lanchester died along with its owner's dream of dominating the world of the quality small saloon.

Engineer Jean-Albert Gregoire stands proud with his new baby, the Hotchkiss-Gregoire, in 1950. It was an adventurous and futuristic saloon featuring front-wheel drive and many fine features, but Hotchkiss simply gave up car-making in 1954, and the car became history.

built up over at least fifty years was discarded at the same time.

The French had been abandoning their motoring heritage quite wantonly throughout the 1950s. Companies like Hotchkiss, Delahaye, Talbot and Rosengart either went bust or just stopped making cars, and there were no entrepreneurs or bargain-hunters waiting in the wings to take them over. The

demise of Borgward was an altogether sadder affair. The German company, renowned for its range of well-made and sporting cars, quite simply spent all its available money on too many different models. In 1961 the company fell apart, mired in a financial crisis from which it could not escape. This was a pity, because its latest product, the Borgward 6 with trendy styling and a novel air-

Another long-lost French marque, Rosengart actually started in business by making the British Austin Seven under licence. After the Second World War it lost its way and there were few takers in those franc-strapped times for this, the SuperTrahuit of 1947, a big luxury saloon with a Ford V8 engine. By 1955 it was all over for Rosengart.

The inner secrets of the impressive 1958 Borgward Six included a complex and sophisticated air suspension system, but such technical delights were not enough to prevent a debt-burdened and over-stretched Borgward from lurching into bankruptcy in 1961.

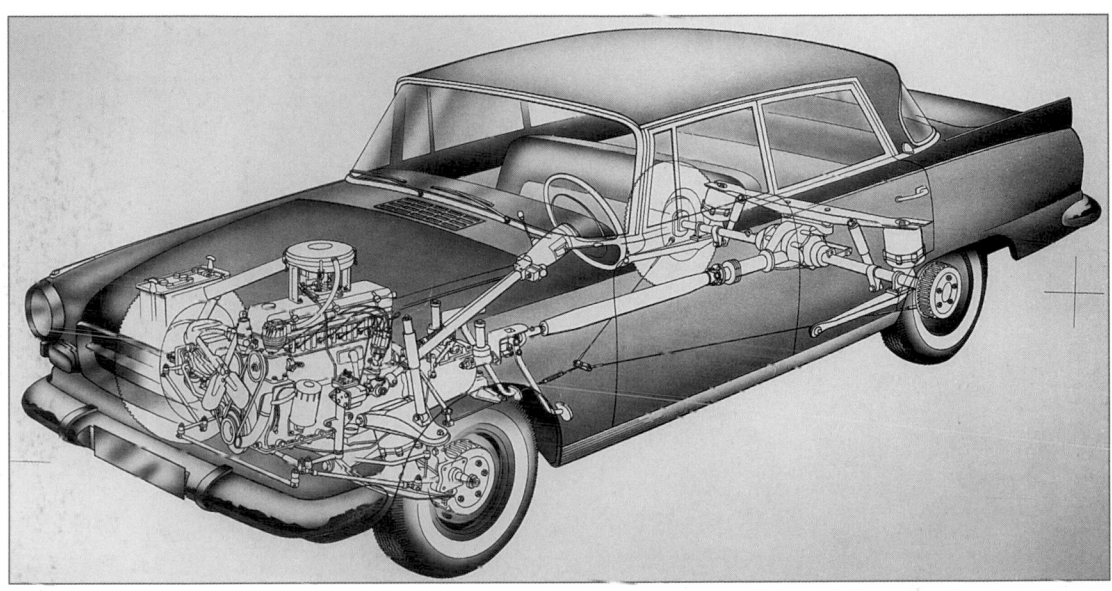

Sharing exhibition space at the Lille Fair in 1959 with scooters and Esperanto books, the Rootes Group showed off its Hillman, Humber and Sunbeam products. Along with Singer, these were all famous marques kept alive by new owners but, after Chrysler took over the British company, all of them were dead by 1976 – maybe, some thought, not before time.

suspension system, had just been launched to great acclaim. Herr Borgward died in 1963, a broken and defeated man.

Humber, Hillman, Singer, Sunbeam – all makes of car that were once revered but are now no longer with us. You can't blame the Rootes family, whose company acquired these august names over a period of thirty years. While rationalising production, they kept these marques alive on a wide range of new Rootes-era cars. The plan went awry, however, after the Americans poked their noses in. In 1964 Chrysler began its takeover of Rootes, and the end was soon in sight for Singer (1970) and later its three siblings (1976) as the dead hand of the Chrysler brand spread itself over everything that the old company now made in the UK. The cars were crap anyway, but it was still a pity.

The last Triumph, on the other hand, was a highly significant car. The Acclaim was the first Japanese-designed car to be built in Britain. It was really a Honda Ballade in all but title, launched in 1981 to generally warm reviews after a long succession of lacklustre British Leyland fare. Three years on and it was decreed that the Rover name was more aspirational than the Triumph one. And that was it: another marque made extinct, another footnote in motoring history.

MOST
USEFUL

OUT OF 10

9th

After the fall of communism and the division of Czechoslovakia into the Czech Republic and Slovakia, the customers for the Tatra 613 – government officials and party high-ups – simply vanished, and no number of facelifts or special models, like this mobile office version, could tempt the nouveaux riche away from their new Mercedes-Benzes.

The Triumph name seemed set for a new lease of life adorning Honda models like the Acclaim, built under licence by a slowly sinking British Leyland. Yet the Acclaim – seen here being bolted together in the Cowley factory where now the new Mini comes from – was only around for three years before Rover was deemed more aspirational.

The vanishing goes on all the time. Tatra, although no longer producing cars, would probably still be happy to make just one more T613 if you really wanted it. Similarly, Italy's De Tomaso has almost ground to a halt, making extreme sports cars in tiny numbers. It did have a Porsche-rivalling sports car on the drawing board, the Bigua, but this project – through a convoluted route of sell-outs and takeovers – has been acquired by MG Rover and will form the basis of the new MG X80 coupé.

Other famous models that have appeared just to peter out include the Lotus Elan, whose manufacturing paraphernalia was sold to a Korean firm, after which it was never heard of again, and, indeed, the Rolls-Royce Silver

The last major car design project initiated by the venerable Alessandro de Tomaso was the front-engined Bigua, with a BMW engine. It subsequently became the Ford V8-engined Qvale Mangusta but now, through a twist of corporate fate, the car is set to form the basis of a new MG luxury sports car.

The caption to this picture reads simply 'Kia Sports Car'. But most enthusiasts would recognise it as the Lotus Elan. The entire production apparatus for the ill-starred, front-wheel drive Elan was sold to Korea in 1992, but Kia only made a few before it succumbed to financial meltdown.

The unseemly carve-up of Rolls-Royce and Bentley between, respectively, BMW and Volkswagen created a poignant casualty in the all-new Rolls-Royce Silver Seraph. VW hastily re-installed the traditional British V8 in its Bentley version, the Arnage, but the BMW-engined Seraph became a bastard child few wealthy buyers wanted to be associated with. It's not a bad car, though.

Honda has rarely made a bad car, but the 1300 was an exception. By order of company founder Soichiro Honda its engine was air-cooled, but customers recoiled at this noisy if practical configuration and, for Mr Honda, it became the last car on which he had any design influence.

Seraph, the final, ill-starred model from the British firm before it was carved up and sold to the Germans.

There can, however, be few 'last-chance saloons' as all-round embarrassing as the Honda 1300. The Japanese company had been built on the engineering brilliance of its founder, Soichiro Honda, whose mopeds put the late twentieth-century world on wheels, and whose cars went down a storm with people who liked products that worked properly. The 1300 was Soichiro's answer to those who wanted a family saloon. However, he would not listen to his fellow directors when they tried to steer him away from giving the car an air-cooled engine. Unveiled in 1968 and in many ways an excellent vehicle, the 1300 and its noisy and unfashionable power unit met with considerable customer resistance, just as the Honda board had feared. It was an expensive mistake, and the company went back to the drawing board to work on what would become the Honda Civic and Accord. The 'old man' was gently but firmly eased into an early retirement in 1973. Possibly sadly for him, Honda the company never looked back.

ONE LAST, GLORIOUS ASSAULT ON THE MIGHTY DETROIT BIG GUYS

Hudson, founded in 1909, was among the last of the American 'independents' – car makers who struggled and ultimately failed in the face of the mighty Ford, General Motors and Chrysler.

Although its cars during the 1920s and '30s were pretty unremarkable – with the exception of its 'Electric Hand' automatic gearbox – Hudson shocked the burghers of Detroit in 1948 with its new range of 'Step Down' cars.

Not only were they sleek and handsome, but their unitary construction featured rear wheels mounted actually inside the chassis frame. There was also independent front suspension.

The range began with the budget-priced Pacemaker and worked its way up through the Super Six, Hornet and

Showing its dramatic lines to good effect, this 1951 example of the Hudson Commodore is one of the few in the UK, in this case as a treasure in the Yorkshire Car Collection.

MAD for it!

Wonderful teardrop-shaped styling, by Frank Spring, made the Hudson seem way ahead of the opposition in 1948, and these interesting cars had a terrific reputation for quality. They are keenly collected in the USA, although almost never encountered in the UK or Europe, more's the pity for lovers of classic Americana.

The Hudson Hornet, similar to the Commodore but with a six-cylinder engine. These three female enthusiasts are no doubt discussing the car's unusual chassis, with the rear wheels inside the frame.

Wasp to the opulent Commodore with Hudson's traditional 4.2-litre straight-eight engine. A brand new 5-litre straight-six cylinder introduced in 1951 for the Hornet boasted 145bhp and made the car a force to be reckoned with in American stock car racing.

But for sheer glamour a Hudson Super Wasp Hollywood hardtop coupé was hard to beat.

Over 145,000 Hudsons were sold in 1950 but the 'Big Three' majors took no hostages when it came to stiff competition. In 1954 Hudson merged with Nash to form American Motors, and in 1957 the venerable Hudson marque was dead.

 SAD for it!

Er – hello! Wheels inside the chassis: what was all that about, then? The Commodore and its Hudson cronies might have looked space-age but what was underneath was pretty ancient – especially the straight-eight engine with its roots in the early 1930s – and their glory was always destined to be shortlived.

The almost impossibly glamorous Hudson Wasp Hollywood hardtop coupé, introduced in 1952, boasted a height of 'only' 5ft.

MOST ATTRACTIVE

OUT OF 10

3rd

THE ISOTTA FRASCHINI
MONTEROSA IN DETAIL

Built: 1947-48 in Milan,
Italy
Engine: V8, 2980cc
Top speed: unknown
Sold in the UK? No
Number made: 6

ITALY'S GREATEST MARQUE AND ITS FANTASTIC FINAL FLING

The Isotta Fraschini marque has had a history of short bursts of glory. In the early part of the century it was Italy's second largest car maker after Fiat, making a range of sporting, aristocratic machines. After the First World War it based all its designs around a fabulous straight-eight engine and its cars became some of the most expensive and exclusive in Europe. But car-making petered out in 1936 as the company's other speciality, ship and aero engines, took over.

One of just a half-dozen prototypes for the Isotta Fraschini Monterosa of 1947, this streamlined open tourer disguised the car's key feature – a V8 engine concealed in its tapering tail.

The Monterosa of 1947 was an attempt to restart car-making. It was an enormous luxury car with a 2.9-litre V8 engine mounted at the back, and the first few built had their cross-shaped chassis clothed in dramatic fashion by some of Italy's finest coachbuilders. This aerodynamic convertible belies its near-half-century age and was designed by Boneschi – still in business today making truck bodies.

But the Italian state, by then in control, decreed Isotta Fraschini must stick to making industrial engines and shut the fledgling Monterosa project down unceremoniously after a year and just half a dozen had been built.

Large Isotta Fraschini power units continue to be made to this day. However, ambitious plans were announced to relaunch Isotta cars in collaboration with Audi in 1998, so renewed glory could still happen.

MAD for it! Here is one of the most glorious might-have-beens in post-war European motoring history. The Monterosa was undoubtedly an interesting car, and could have been a big hit – especially in the USA – had the company's Italian paymasters the guts to stick with this advanced design.

SAD for it! Enormous rear-engined slug was hardly the right car for post-war Italy, despite the excellence of Isotta Fraschini's reputation. Production never began and, although there is reverence for the early days of the marque, can you really see Isotta, revived on a shoestring, competing with the likes of Lexus and Mercedes-Benz?

A more recent Isotta Fraschini prototype was the T8 shown here, a luxurious sports car with Audi power and four-wheel drive; despite optimistic noises, the car has yet to actually go on sale.

Built: 1957 in Coventry, West Midlands
Engine: six-cylinder, 3442cc
Top speed: 150mph
Sold in the UK? Yes
Number made: 16

THE D-TYPE SET LE MANS ALIGHT BUT THE XKSS NEVER LEFT THE GRID

The night of 12 February 1957 started normally enough at Jaguar's Coventry factory. The last workers cycled home through the gates; the nightwatchman settled down with the local paper. But by morning a raging inferno had ripped across the Browns Lane works, scorching its way through everything in its path. Around 270 cars were destroyed, among them many examples of the scintillating new XKSS.

Launched just weeks before the blaze, the XKSS looked pretty much like the Le Mans-winning Jaguar D-type. Not surprisingly, really, as it was merely a roadgoing version of the racer with decent seats, wind-up windows, bumpers and a hood. Jaguar had withdrawn from competition and this was its novel ruse to use up unsold D-types and, perhaps, put the XKSS into production as a proper sports car.

Taken from a catalogue, this evocative artwork for the XKSS can't disguise its D-type roots, despite the carefully added hood, bumpers and practical luggage rack.

CLEVEREST FEATURES

OUT OF 10

7th

How it looks in real life: this example of the XKSS was once owned and driven by Hollywood star Steve McQueen, and was latterly restored by Lynx Motors.

Nine gutted XKSSs were still smouldering in the cold light of that February morning; some had literally melted away as their aluminium bodywork was fanned by the intense heat. Only 16 had reached customers and, as Jaguar poured its all into rebuilding the factory, the 250bhp XKSS was put on the backburner – forever.

Yet it wasn't all bad news: the car was a direct ancestor of the fabled 1961 E-type.

The Jaguar sports car line-up as the company would like to have it, with the XKSS a vital missing link; an XK8 is in front with behind it (left to right) the SS100, XK120, E-type and XJ-S.

The XKSS did not perish in vain: it was the inspiration for the sensational 1961 E-type, seen here in a period advertisement on the cover of *Autocar* magazine.

MAD for it!

What a car: a genuine, road-going version of the D-type, an out-and-out racing car that had won Le Mans three times in a row between 1955 and 1957. Phenomenally fast and rather furious, you would have had to be a bit of a he-man to drive it, but who cared: it was still the most exciting British sports car of its day.

SAD for it!

It can't have been fun seeing the Browns Lane plant go up in smoke, taking scores of Jags with it, but at least the raucous XKSS was stopped in its tracks: with a fresh start forced on the company, work began on the E-type – the car that would define sporting Jaguars thereafter.

With its hat-trick of victories at Le Mans, the Jaguar D-type, seen here at a recent Goodwood Festival, was the stuff of legends, and the basis of the ill-fated XKSS.

Autocar

JAGUAR 'E' TYPE
The most advanced sports car in the world

NUBAR GULBENKIAN'S
LONDON TAXI IN
DETAIL

Built: 1965 in Coventry,
West Midlands and
Battersea, south-west
London
Engine: four-cylinder,
2199cc
Top speed: unknown
Sold in the UK? No
Number made: 1

IT TURNED ON A SIXPENCE – WHATEVER THAT WAS

UGLIEST
CAR

OUT OF 10

5th

The thoroughly weird shape created by FLM Panelcraft for Nubar Gulbenkian appeared to weld a taxi nose on to the front of a Victorian hansom cab. Still, he liked it.

MAD for it!

If it wasn't for the imagination – not to say the readies – of people like Nubar Gulbenkian, then the car world would be a duller place. And, when you think about it, a wacky luxury limo with the practical advantages of a London cab actually makes a lot of sense.

FLM created another unique car for Gulbenkian when it turned a standard Rolls-Royce Silver Cloud into this 'sedanca deville' limo, complete with hooded headlights and tiny rear tailfins.

Nubar Sarkis Gulbenkian, monocle in his right eye and orchid always on his lapel, was one of London's most recognisable playboys. He lived at the Ritz, whiled many an hour away at the St James Club, married three times and enjoyed a tycoon's lifestyle.

He was an oil mogul. Like his father before him, the Armenian Jew Calouste Gulbenkian, Nubar had helped develop the UK's oil interests in the Middle East. Old Calouste's acumen at deal-making earned him the nickname 'Mr Five Per Cent'; Nubar was no less astute, but spent more time enjoying his vast fortune than dad ever had.

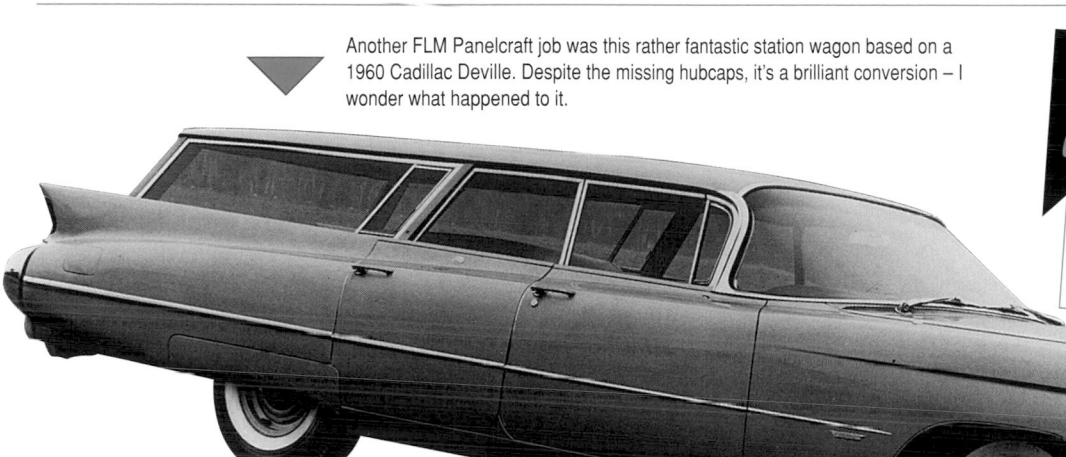

Another FLM Panelcraft job was this rather fantastic station wagon based on a 1960 Cadillac Deville. Despite the missing hubcaps, it's a brilliant conversion – I wonder what happened to it.

SAD for it! This has to be one of the worst stylistic mis-matches of all time, and just think of the cash the London dandy must have laid out for it. He had little grasp of money: it was this vehicle about which Nubar Gulbenkian coined the phrase: 'It'll turn on a sixpence – whatever that is.'

And what did he spend it on? The good life, sure, and cars. At first it was ultra-fast vintage supercars; then a string of specially made and mostly very ugly Rolls-Royces.

But, weary of the usual rich men's playthings, Nubar decided to have a special miniature limousine built – based on London's superbly manoeuvrable taxi. It was carefully constructed in 1965 to his design by a Battersea coachbuilder, and incorporated gold-plated fittings, a glass Lalique bonnet mascot and a rear end that looked as if a horse-drawn brougham had simply been welded on to the nose of a black cab.

It was one of London's most famous cars but Gulbenkian died in 1972, aged 72, and his precious one-off taxi went to California. It still exists, and made £23,000 at an auction a few years ago.

The FX4 London Taxi, once an Austin, then Carbodies-badged and in the end (shown here) called an LTI Fairway, had an amazingly long life, introduced in 1958 and replaced – not before time – in 1997.

MAD OFF-ROADERS

Some of these mud-pluggers have dirty secrets

I apologise in advance if you work on a farm or need to get around a large building site on a regular basis, but let's face it: the nearest that most drivers of off-road vehicles come to actually leaving the highway in them is when they mount the kerb in error while parking at Tesco's. A few dedicated souls may tow a horse-box or traverse a bit of wet grass, but the majority of these four-wheel drive creatures are owned for show rather than go.

You could, I suppose, blame Alfa Romeo for starting this absurd trend. After the Second World War the Milan-

MOST ATTRACTIVE

OUT OF 10

7th

MOST SURPRISING

OUT OF 10

1st

A truly odd sight: it might look like a Jeep but this is actually an Alfa Romeo 1900 AR52 4x4 military vehicle, and here it is just about to win its class on the 1953 Mille Miglia road race – an event more readily associated with exotica like Ferrari and Maserati.

This is a Rayton Fissore Magnum, a sort of Italian Range Rover wth a military-derived chassis and a leather-trimmed interior thanks to craftsmen at one of Italy's long-established coachbuilders. It's still available, although these days it wears the LaForza badge.

based sports car maker also did a neat line in Jeep-like military vehicles. One of these, a 1900 AR52, was entered into the 1953 Mille Miglia road race. It was no joke: despite the presence of the cream of the world's racing-sports cars, the rugged Alfa won its class. Ever since, 4x4 owners have sought to make just as bold a statement on the road.

Three other bizarre Italian off-roaders spring to mind. The Rayton Fissore

One of the strangest off-roaders to emerge from Italy in recent times came from Lamborghini. The LM002 could make short work of anything from tropical jungle to desert dunes thanks, of course, to its four-wheel drive but also the massive power from its Countach-derived engine. It was, briefly, the darling of the Middle East chic set.

Magnum was a real case of silk purse from sow's ear. Its basis was an Iveco military truck, but the 1986 car was given a chic new outfit by the old-established Fissore coachworks. The man who designed this was Tom Tjaarda, who had also been responsible for the De Tomaso Mangusta and the Ford Fiesta, and a descendant of the Magnum called the LaForza is still manufactured for those who want it. These Latin interpretations of the Range Rover have never really captured buyers' imaginations.

Which can't be said of the Lamborghini LM002. Originally launched as the Lamborghini Cheetah, this enormous mud-plugger put the company's near-legendary V12 engine in the hands of determined terrain bashers. As the LM002, it was a favourite of Arab sheiks, Texas oil barons, and horsepower-mad schoolboys during its short production life. There will, almost certainly, never be another Lamborghini quite like it.

And then there was the batty 1991 Bertone Freeclimber, a Daihatsu Sportrak assembled in Turin and given a BMW power unit. This amalgam of bits and pieces sounds bizarre and was a total disaster among customers.

Still, there have been more outrageous off-roaders than this trio. Unique

A more bizarre amalgam of automotive bits and pieces it would be hard to imagine: the Bertone Freeclimber was launched in 1992, uniting the body of a Daihatsu Sportrak with a BMW engine, and the whole thing was assembled in Italy. It was a commercial disaster, and never imported to the UK.

The cartoonish lines of the Sbarro Windhound, hailing from Switzerland in 1981, intended to shock and delight in about equal measure. Its designer Franco Sbarro is at the wheel and, indeed, is still turning out left-field cars that entertain motor show visitors year after year.

The man who designed this wedge-shaped mud-basher, Dennis Adams, was also responsible for the classic Marcos sports car, would you believe. It's called the Glenfrome Facet, was launched in 1982, built in Bristol, and underneath those look-at-me clothes was the chassis of the Range Rover.

designers and craftmen. Their work has spanned the truly outrageous – such as the Glenfrome Facet of 1982, a sort of high-riding sports coupé with removable roof panels from the pen of Marcos stylist Dennis Adams – to the utterly functional, like the many hunting vehicles produced by London-based FLM Panelcraft for myriad wealthy, and mostly Arab, big game aficionados. However, it is still possible to purchase a truly functional off-roader. In China they make nothing else. The Beijing is the country's staple 4x4, as rough-edged as an aerial photo of the Great Wall of China but, none the less, just the job for everything from rounding up dissidents in Red Square to harassing the odd Tibetan monk on remote mountainsides. Likewise, the UMM, which has been in production for many years in Portugal, is strictly for the hardcore negotiator of the rough stuff. While Land-Rover lists options such as leather seats and DVD players, a more typical accessory for a UMM would be a winch, a snowplough or breathing apparatus for those high altitudes.

On the other side of the world, off-road ruggedness can be obtained in a variety of ways. Generations of Brazilians have gone about their demanding rural tasks in a variety of Gurgels, such as the Xavante, a line of Volkswagen-powered four-wheel drive buggies, many of which have been converted to run on alcohol-derived fuel.

And further north, of course, we have the Hummer. It's been around since

creations from bespoke car customisers around Europe have regularly popped up over the last three decades. The Swiss designer Franco Sbarro has produced a steady stream of four-wheel drive oddities such as the Windhound, usually built on a cost-no-object basis. The engines and drivetrain may have

been hijacked from other vehicles but the flamboyant style was something else entirely. Britain's own bespoke 4x4 industry has long centred around the Range Rover. Countless elongated, chopped, extravagantly trimmed and ultra-powerful interpretations of Solihull's finest have been created by ingenious

1990, and is familiar around the world as one of the US Army's most versatile assets in conflicts such as the 1991 Gulf War. Wider than a three-seater sofa, and boasting a huge 6.2-litre V8 diesel engine, the Hummer is perhaps the ultimate go-anywhere vehicle. The company makes some 1,000 civilian editions each year, which have been bought by larger-than-life drivers like Arnold Schwarzenegger. Now that General Motors has bought AM General, the Hummer manufacturer, a more tarmac-friendly incarnation has been developed: the smaller, but still immense, Hummer H2 has at the time of writing just gone on sale.

A Range Rover hunting vehicle converted by London specialist FLM Panelcraft in about 1984. You probably get the idea of what this car was for simply by seeing its upholstery, but the sober green paint, plain wheels and fold-flat windscreen are restrained by comparison with many of its customised ilk.

UGLIEST
CAR
OUT OF 10
1st

The Beijing is China's standard-issue off-road workhorse, assigned to all manner of duties across this vast land, including the odd bit of bother with local freedom fighters. Its internationally unacceptable crudeness has hampered exports, although this one got the slow boat to Britain for a shakedown on some testing moorland.

MOST
USEFUL
OUT OF 10
10th

The UMM hails from Portugal and is even more utilitarian than a Land Rover Defender. They've been making them like this for years, and UMMs are to be found in such unglamorous locations as building sites and road construction areas all over southern Europe.

And what about going one stage further than off-road? The waterborne car has long had a fascination to the general public, perhaps dating back to the Second World War when German DUKW amphibious vehicles intrigued the British armed forces. The only com-mercially successful seagoing car so far has been the Amphicar, a German-built but Triumph Herald-engined device which has been proved to be able to cross the English Channel, but is undoubtedly more at home in the middle of Rutland Water. A modern take on the amphibious car that looked set for success was the 1993 Hobbycar, a neat and, happy to say, extremely buoyant vehicle, boasting not only a marinised Peugeot engine but also twin propellers. Sadly, the enterprise appears to have sunk without trace. . . .

A Gurgel Xavante X12 flies through the air just above the South American tundra; these Volkswagen-based four-wheel drive buggies have long been a part of the Brazilian motoring scene, offering a winning combination of go-anywhere ruggedness and VW reliability.

Familiar around the world thanks to TV news reports of conflicts in the Gulf War and, recently, Afghanistan, the Hummer is truly unmistakable. Some 1,000 a year are bought by private individuals with a point to make, but watch out for the new, more consumer-friendly Hummer now that General Motors has bought AM General, the company that makes it.

MOST USELESS
OUT OF 10
5th

UGLIEST CAR
OUT OF 10
3rd

'Off-road' doesn't necessarily mean just 'off-tarmac'. The 1993 Hobbycar was a French effort at making a seagoing car acceptable, with a neat design and marinised Peugeot diesel power. How far you'd dare to go in one, of course, is another matter: I don't think one ever crossed the Channel, for instance.

MOST USEFUL
OUT OF 10
5th

Built: 1930-40 in
Friedrichschafen,
Germany
Engine: V12, 7977cc
Top speed: 103mph
Sold in the UK? Yes
Number made: 250
approx

RESISTANCE IS FUTILE: VE VILL BUILD EUROPE'S BIGGEST CAR

Its bonnet alone measured 7ft, a Ford Fiesta could park *within* its 12ft wheelbase, its radiator was 3ft wide and the car weighed well over 3 tons. Not for nothing was Maybach's claim to be Germany's king of cars unchallenged – even by Mercedes-Benz. Wilhelm Maybach partnered Gottlieb Daimler in designing the very earliest cars but split in 1907, with his son Karl, to produce engines for Count Zeppelin's airships. A magnificent V12 car motor was a natural progression and, when no car maker would take up the challenge to fit it in their products, Maybach designed his own.

Between 1921 and 1941 fewer than 2,000 Maybach cars were sold, but they were phenomenally expensive, beautifully finished and near-silent – and, in Britain, gained the nickname of the 'German Rolls-Royce'; the German ambassador in London used one. Like Rolls, Maybach made only chassis – customers could have any bodywork they fancied.

The quite extraordinary Maybach Zeppelin with aerodynamic body designed by streamlining genius Paul Jaray. How would you cope with a 7ft long bonnet?

MAD for it! For Maybach buyers, a Mercedes-Benz was just too flashy, yet – as most of them were wealthy and conservative Germans – patriotism forbade them from considering a Rolls-Royce or a Pierce-Arrow. Enormous, imposing and soon to reappear, in spirit, thanks to Mercedes-Benz.

The aerodynamic behemoth you see here, called the Maybach Zeppelin, was probably the ultimate, its bodywork custom-built by Spohn of Ravensburg and designed by the leading aerodynamicist Paul Jaray, and its driver enjoying an eight-speed gearbox.

In the Germany of 1945, however, there was no place for a leviathan like the Zeppelin, and the marque became history – or so everyone thought. In fact, it was acquired by Mercedes-Benz which long nursed a secret dream of resuscitating it. This happened in 2001 when the new Maybach was unveiled, an awe-inspiring luxury model intended for royally and film stars. It should be on sale by 2004 but its phenomenal cost and exclusivity mean you'll be unlikely to see one on the North Circular.

Mercedes-Benz had long dreamed of reviving the Maybach marque, and in 2001 it revealed its thinking with a truly enormous luxury limousine. The reworked Maybach badge, however, is the only tangible link.

☹ SAD for it!

This car was big in every way. Not that the owners would have realised: their chauffeurs would have had to cope with the 7ft-long bonnet and eye-widening turning circle while their masters lounged in the back, no doubt plotting their doomed European domination.

At well north of £200,000, the new Maybach is destined to be as exclusive as its 1930s antecedents; whether the imposing style has quite the same impact, though, is questionable – the new one is pretty restrained.

S:MY 729D

THE MERCEDES-BENZ
200/CONTINENTAL
'DRIVERLESS' CAR IN
DETAIL

Built: 1968 in Stuttgart,
Germany
Engine: four-cylinder,
2197cc
Top speed: unknown
Sold in the UK? No
Number made: 1

WHY BUY A MERC AND DRIVE YOURSELF?

The 'driverless' car has been something of an alchemy quest: relaxing in your personalised cocoon while neither driving nor employing a chauffeur is a concept that's kept many an automotive egghead awake at night. Tyre-maker Continental, though, actually pioneered one back in 1968, an outwardly normal Mercedes saloon boasting a boot jam-packed with computer equipment.

Look, mum, no hands! Continental's specially made Merc thunders around the Contidrome test track as if, says the caption to this picture, 'controlled by a ghostly hand'.

MAD for it! There can be few drivers who haven't got sick of crawling along in traffic, or exhausted after many long hours pounding the motorway. Continental offered an alternative to all that, and its primitive technology, if developed, could have proved a world beater with a little imagination – and the help of the autobahn authorities.

Even on a banked circuit, the modified Mercedes-Benz 200 had no need for human assistance, no doubt cutting the cost of tyre-testing for Continental.

Werkbild: Continental

Up-close on how it worked: the Mercedes received its driving instructions from a computer-controlled guide cable installed in the concrete of the test track.

DAFTEST FEATURES
OUT OF 10
5th

The view from the driver's seat as seen by, well, absolutely nobody. However, controllers at the Contidrome's test centre could monitor every centimetre the car travelled on its own.

With a controller in a tower at the company's 'Contidrome' test track in Germany, the automatic Mercedes could spend many a contented day bowling round and round the circuit, its two measuring coils mounted on the front bumper reading the magnetic field of a cable embedded in the concrete track.

When it sensed the car was veering off course, on a bend or in a sidewind, an electric message sent to the helm corrected the steering, as if some unseen ghost were at the wheel.

The car never left the traffic-free confines of Continental's test centre, of course, where it dutifully wore its rubber out all day without needing stops for coffee and fags. Indeed, no-one has since refined the idea of a hands-free car for the public highway. When it comes to unmanned vehicles, the Docklands Light Railway is still about as close as you can get.

SAD for it!

What, I ask you, is the point of a car that drives itself? The words dog, buy, yourself and bark come to mind, not necessarily in that order. If you don't want to drive then take a train – don't snooze in the back of your Merc while unnerving other drivers as they panic at your driverless car. . . .

THE MIELE IN DETAIL

Built: 1911-13 in Guetersloh, Germany
Engine: four-cylinder, 1568/2292cc
Top speed: unknown
Sold in the UK? No
Number made: 125

HUNT FOR ITS MISSING 'APPLIANCE' PUT MIELE IN A SPIN

A Miele washing machine or dishwasher is a must-have for every smart kitchen. Expensive jeans from Cannes to Chester wouldn't be caught spinning in anything less. But in 1912 the German founders of Miele, Carl Miele and Reinhard Zinkann, were convinced they could also make the king of cars.

Five be-hatted German motoring enthusiasts, salivating slightly at the prospect of a day out in a Miele car; the marque had an excellent reputation for quality, although just 125 were sold.

MAD for it!

Bet you never knew there was a link between that ridiculously expensive dishwasher you've just shelled out for – on the advice of your interior designer – and the world of cars. The Miele was a handsome machine, and it's a credit to the firm that it takes enough pride in its heritage to track one down for its archives.

Rudolph Miele (at the wheel) and Dr Peter Zinkann in the recently restored Miele car, found in a Norwegian shed and now a much-prized corporate heirloom.

Introduced in 1912, the Miele K1 tourer boasted a 17bhp four-cylinder engine. German car magazine *Stahlrad und Automobil* said: 'No other automobile factory has achieved the same success in such a short time as Miele.' A bigger 22bhp K2 model soon joined it, together with a long-wheelbase limousine said to cost what the mayor of Guetersloh, Miele's home town, earned in a year.

They were exported as far afield as Brazil and Russia, but after 125 cars had been built in two years Miele decided its future was with the household appliances it built alongside them.

It was assumed all examples of Miele cars had driven into the mists of time. But Rudolph Miele and Peter Zinkann, the descendants of the founders who still own the private firm, yearned to find one. A remarkably original survivor eventually turned up in Norway after a five-year hunt; it had led a hard life as a taxi and a driving school car but now rubs wheelnuts with early wooden washing machines in Miele's museum.

The early Miele cars looked very unconventional. I jest, of course: this is actually an early Miele washing machine, the gadget with which the German manufacturer has come to worldwide prominence.

MOST SURPRISING

OUT OF 10

5th

SAD for it!

What a pity the company didn't stick with cars. If its 'white goods' manufactured today are anything to go by then Miele cars would probably have had a bright future as yet another high-quality German marque. If you find one in your Uncle Heinrich's shed, you'll own the only other surviving example known to man.

Built: 1973 in Leamington Spa, West Midlands

Engine: four-cylinder, 998cc

Top speed: unknown

Sold in the UK? No

Number made: 1

THE NEWEST MINI WAS WEDGE-SHAPED – WELL, IT WAS 1973

Two years ago, an all-new Mini was unveiled that, while nowhere near as revolutionary and endearing as the original in 1959, still achieved the near-impossible: it got 'ordinary' people – that is to say, non-car fanatics – excited by small cars once again. But thoughts have turned to a 'New Mini' many times before. The car's creator Sir Alec Issigonis had a crack at it in the late 1960s with a little hatchback code-named 9X, and the Minissima was a promising reinterpretation in 1973.

MOST WEDGE-SHAPED OUT OF 10

5th

The Minissima was a vision of how a British small car of the 1970s might look. There are no doors at the side, just a single one at the back.

MAD for it! With British Leyland's design in periodic stagnation during the 1970s, it was left to freelance designers like Towns to point the Mini to the future. The rear entry was radical but the shape proved prescient – is there not something of the highly-successful Mercedes-Benz A-Class in the Minissima's overall proportions?

Designer William Towns, seemingly imprisoned inside the Minissima, was very much the car design man of the moment in 1973, having designed the Aston Martin DBS and Jensen-Healey.

The severe-lined 'one-box' car packed the Mini's venerable A-Series engine, a four-speed automatic gearbox and front-wheel drive into a tiny wheelbase. The Minissima was as long as most cars were wide – so short was it, in fact, that it could be parked end-on to the kerb. You could safely disembark straight on to the pavement through the car's only door, sited centrally at the back.

The Minissima was the work of the late designer William Towns, best known for styling the Aston Martin DBS and Lagonda. British Leyland couldn't summon up the gumption necessary to make and market such a radical runabout, but the design eventually bore fruit for Towns: a bicycle maker called Elswick renamed it the Envoy, widened the rear door, added doors at the side and found a niche for the Minissima – as a car into which the wheelchair-bound driver could easily whizz and instantly set off.

Towns later came up with a car even more compact than the Minissima. The tiny Microdot had a three-cylinder Daihatsu engine and was built in 1980.

The Minissima did finally make it on to the market. Made by the Elswick bicycle company, it was sold as the Envoy and was intended as the ideal car for the wheelchair-bound driver.

CLEVEREST FEATURES
OUT OF 10
8th

SAD for it!
This was always going to be a car you'd be stared at in. This was fine for its time as a publicity-gaining design exercise, but not so pleasant for the wheelchair-bound who became the ultimate users of the Minissima when it went into limited production.

MAD STRETCHES

Some people will go to any lengths for a limousine

The British car industry has just spent £5m on congratulating Her Majesty the Queen on reaching her Golden Jubilee. Bentley Motors corralled a consortium of suppliers and designers into building the monarch a magnificent limousine that will not only keep her in the public gaze when she is on the move, but will also preserve her elderly frame behind bullet-proof glass and armour plating. The car is a total one-off – and one of the longest passenger cars to be built in Britain for many years.

A gift from the British motor industry to the Queen in her Golden Jubilee year, this Bentley State Limousine cost some £5m to build and has rendered her creaking Rolls-Royce Phantom VI somewhat redundant. Magnificent though it is, however, wouldn't a maroon and black Ford Mondeo be just as useful?

MOST USELESS

OUT OF 10

2nd

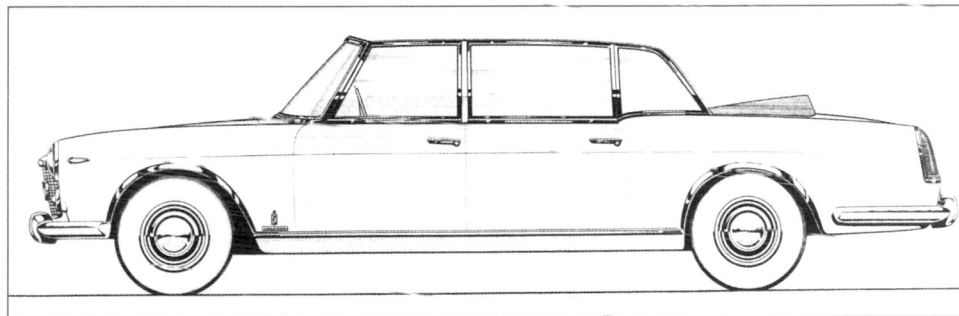

Quite why this gargantuan Bentley needs to be so long is, when you think about it, a bit baffling. When she is out on parade, the Queen never travels with more than one companion, usually Prince Philip. And, of course, a chauffeur and a bodyguard always travel up-front. A Ford Mondeo with a glass roof could perform exactly the same duty at a mere fraction of the cost. But that would be to miss the point of this piece of rolling, celebratory opulence. She is the Queen, after all: if she can't lord it over us on the motorway, then who can?

Not so much a stretch as a purely enormous motor car, this extraordinary Rolls-Royce Phantom VI convertible began life as a one-off special designed by Pietro Frua in Italy but ended up being completed and sold by David Royle, a County Durham-based vintage car restorer. It was last seen on a Geneva motor show stand in the early 1990s.

Bizarrely, it was Queen Elizabeth II who sparked the design of this stretched Lancia Flaminia, commissioned from Pininfarina in 1961 by President Giovanni Gronchi for her state visit to Italy. The seven-seater cabriolet was the first new addition to the Italian government fleet since 1931.

The bloke on the plane steps clearly isn't a US president, but the giant-sized stretched Cadillac from 1988 is called the Presidential Limousine, and appears to have enough headroom for the elaborate headgear of any visiting foreign dignitary.

'Very Important People' have long used excessive length to impart their image of prestige and power. You might have expected it from US presidents like Ronald Reagan, swanning along the avenues of Washington DC in an enormous Cadillac. But in Cold War Russia, despite the Communist regime, the limousines were just as big and just as brash. Actually, the 1956 ZIL was

In Russia there used to be special lanes reserved for Communist Party officials down which giant black-painted ZIL 114s like these would speed. Massive in weight, bulk and cost, these enormous V8 limousines are still built as a sideline by a Moscow truck factory, and still favoured by Putin as official transport.

The typical British stretched limo has been the sort of car most people dread – something to carry grieving relatives to funerals. This one is a rare beast, an Austin 3-litre elongated by Halifax artisans Woodall Nicholson in about 1970, and is as sombre looking as most of its type.

Coleman Milne have been cutting and lengthening Fords for some forty years, mostly for the funeral trade but also as transport for the chainmail-wearing burghers of local government. This one is from around 1973 and boasts a special bonnet as befits its town hall pomp.

For a time in the 1980s Mercedes-Benz shied away from making lengthened versions of its most expensive models, leaving the market wide open to local specialists like Le Marquis in the UK, which could add a chunk of extra metal of any size you wanted to the S Class. This example is in a Park Lane dealer showroom in 1985.

closely modelled on an American car of the time, a Packard, and ZILs, with their V8 engines and slow of convenience features like automatic transmission, have copied Detroit ever since. In large Russian cities, in those 'red' days, special lanes were provided for government officials and apparatchiks, and a speeding ZIL was the car that used them most.

Away from the arena of world leaders, we perhaps most readily associate stretched cars with marriages and deaths. In Britain we are used to seeing these sombre eight-seaters, created by slicing a humdrum saloon – it started with cars like the Austin 3-litre but these days it's far more likely to be a Ford Scorpio – in half, and inserting a

UGLIEST CAR

OUT OF 10

6th

This somewhat graceless and square-cut stretch began life as a Nissan Laurel, and was turned into a rather forbidding limousine by Glenfrome of Bristol in 1988. It was 36in longer and called the Wessex, but series production of this and a six-door monster version never actually began.

A factory-produced stretch limousine is a rare thing – the demand for a volume model wouldn't be there, manufacturers reason. However, in 1982 Chrysler bucked convention with this seven-seater based on its K-Car compact model, complete with a glass division and two folding 'jump' seats.

custom-made extension. But anything can be stretched: during the late 1980s British specialists took their angle-grinders to all manner of cars, everything from the ritzy Mercedes-Benz S-class, elongated by Jankel, to the risible Nissan Laurel, pulled at both ends by Bristol-based Glenfrome.

However, not all stretched cars have been worked on by outsiders. Chrysler's infamous K-car of 1982 featured a pint-sized limousine as part of the standard range, while Checker, forever associated in the cinematic mind's eye with the traditional New York taxi, marketed its 1962 Aerobus as a catalogue model during the 1960s.

MOST USEFUL

OUT OF 10

2nd

The Checker Aerobus is one of the longest purpose-built passenger cars of all time, a standard, New York taxi-style Checker stretched to 21ft 4in, so turning it into an eight-door, fifteen-seater behemoth suited, I reckon, to transporting large but extremely close-knit families around airport terminals.

It doesn't just have to be saloon cars that are stretched: this Ford Granada estate was given 2 extra feet in its centre section to accommodate Martin and Gaynor Mears, their four sons Toby, Brett, Damian and Alexander, and their two sheepdogs Rupert and Sophie. The conversion was carried out in 1976 by Bolton-based Coleman Milne.

A few extra inches (or centimetres) make all the difference: this is the additional 10cm of metal Skoda inserts between the doors of its Octavia saloon to create the ever-so-slightly lengthened cars for the Czech government, or anyone else who wants a car with that crucial bit of extra rear legroom.

And nor does a car need to be stretched too far to make a real difference to the comfort of its occupants. Skoda, for instance, is mighty proud of the stretched Octavia saloons that have been selected for use by government ministers in the Czech Republic. It's locally made, obviously, but also has 10cm of extra metal let into the centre for that crucial additional luxury.

The stretching business isn't confined to traditionally prosperous markets either. Brazil's Avallone company has made quite a name for itself by sawing cars in half – anything from imported Mercedes-Benzes to locally built Chevrolets and Volkswagens – and selling them to local dignitaries and soap stars.

Here is a stretched limousine from the *other* America. This Chevrolet Opala, one of a wide range of obscure General Motors models built in Brazil, was sawn in half by local specialist Avallone before it was turned into a limo for local Mr Bigs – possibly Ronnie Biggs.

Built: 1954 in Turin, Italy
Engine: four-cylinder, 750cc
Top speed: 133mph
Sold in the UK? No
Number made: 1

DOUBLE TROUBLE AS CARLO'S DREAM CAR HIT A LIGHT BREEZE

Here's a positive catamaran of a car. The Bisiluro has twin 'hulls', with the driver and fuel tank embedded in the right one and the engine and gearbox in the left. Connecting them are a giant, slatted heat exchanger and a clever, two-stage aerodynamic brake. Its streamlined shape was the work of an Italian architect called Carlo Mollino, and it was very, very light.

That engine, a four-cylinder, 750cc unit, gave 65bhp at a screaming 6500rpm and was inspired, admitted its designer Carlo Giannini, by the engine in Moto Guzzi's top racing motorbikes. Constructor Enrico Nardi knew it was ideal for the Bisiluro's task: tackling the 1955 Le Mans 24-hour race with Mollino and a co-pilot called Damonte sharing the arduous driving schedule.

With its twin-hulled body resembling two fat cigars, the Bisiluro was one of the strangest cars to take part at Le Mans in 1955 – sadly, it was one of the non-finishers too.

The driver and fuel were located in the left boom, the engine and gearbox in the right one, while the slatted thing in between them was a giant heat-exchanger.

MAD for it! Not every experiment works, obviously, but hats off to the Italian trio of *signori* Mollino, Giannini and Nardi for creating an arresting racing car that was amazingly fast for such a small engine, and showed much ingenuity in its twin-hulled layout.

In the early 1990s Giannini entered the nostalgia business when it began to sell a plastic replica of the characterful Fiat 500 Abarth, calling it the Corsa 590.

The Giannini company is still very much in business, although these days it specialises in customised versions of standard Fiat cars, like this souped-up Tipo 1600SX Sportline.

SAD for it! The fact that this aerodynamic wonder was actually blown off-course at Le Mans simply because a bigger car overtook it says a lot about how how half-baked the thinking behind it turned out to be. Architects should stick to buildings.

The Bisiluro was incredibly fast, capable of 133mph, and had been averaging a plucky 91mph around the French circuit when disaster struck. A Jaguar overtook at such speed that the ensuing gust of wind forced the Bisiluro off the road and, in doing so, ended its race.

Happily this twin-fuselage oddball has survived, been restored, and is sometimes exhibited by the Giannini company, which is still very much in business as a builder of uprated Fiat cars.

DAFTEST FEATURES

OUT OF 10

7th

In 1972 Giannini also toyed with an ultra-basic four-wheel drive vehicle that could be put to a variety of uses. Not sure if I'd like to drive along with a Fiat 500 suspended over my head, though. . . .

Built: 1989–90 in Yokohama, Japan
Engine: four-cylinder, 988cc
Top speed: 87mph
Sold in the UK? No
Number made: 10,000

WHEN NISSAN DID RETRO, THEY REALLY WENT TO TOWN – TOY TOWN

In the late 1980s hundreds of Mini Coopers, Vanden Plas 1100s, and Renault 4s were appearing in Tokyo's tightly packed car parks. Europe's everyday cars of yesteryear were highly fashionable and worth thousands where they'd make just a few hundred back home. Nissan decided to grab a piece of the action. It built 'The Pike Factory'.

Nissan's ultra-retro Pao city car used such features as exterior door hinges, fold-up windows and round headlights to summon up an earlier, cruder era in small cars typified by the Renault 4.

Nissan's dalliance with the past began with the Be-1, an attractive little car with its round headlights and full-length sunshine roof. It was the first Nissan built at The Pike Factory.

From this mysterious establishment sallied forth a series of lovingly detailed retro-cars like the Be-1, with its round headlamps and soft-top roof, and the idiosyncratic, snail-shaped S-Cargo van.

There was also the 1989 Pao, a sort of lovechild of Fiat Panda, Mini Clubman and Fiat 500 extraction. It bristled with self-consciously dated touches like canvas seats, flip-up side windows, exposed door hinges and ribbed body sides looking like a giant toaster. Japan's chic set loved them and there was an instant months-long waiting list.

Beneath the evocative exterior, though, was nothing more pulsating than a basic Nissan Micra floorpan, engine and automatic gearbox.

Japan can't get enough novelties, and the cheeky, limited-edition Pao was soon ousted as number one must-have by the two-seater Figaro coupé.

Officially 'Pike' cars were never exported but a smattering of Be-1s, S-Cargos and Figaros – one for popster Betty Boo – made it to the UK. Never, apparently, a Pao, though.

The charming little Figaro is the most well known of the 'Pike Factory' cars, a beautifully executed two-seater convertible that sold like hot cakes when it was announced.

😞 **SAD for it!**

Silly: that's the only word for the Pao, S-Cargo, Figaro and Be-1. Nissan dressed up nothing more exciting than the Micra with a series of cartoonish clothes. The Pike Factory interlude is certainly one of the reasons the company was brought to the brink of bankruptcy, only to be rescued by Renault.

The return of curvy lines to small cars did, in fact, reap rewards for Nissan: the very successful new Nissan Micra of 1992 possessed much of the rotund character of the Be-1 and Pao.

☞ **MAD for it!**

Clever old Nissan tapped into Japan's dual 1980s passions for nostalgia and novelty with the Pao and its wacky brethren. Happily these cars were also easy to own and drive thanks to trusty mechanical parts, and the level of detail design never failed to delight their proud owners.

Built: 1962 in Coventry, West Midlands and Letchworth, Hertfordshire
Engine: V8, 2548cc
Top speed: unknown
Sold in the UK? Yes
Number made: 2

OH, MR FORTER: WHAT A LOVELY, ER, OGLE-BODIED DAIMLER

In the hall of the motoring great and good, Boris Forter doesn't figure prominently. Not surprising, really: you wouldn't expect the one-time joint-managing director of the British Helena Rubinstein Company to be much of a car name. Yet it was this patrician captain of cosmetics who helped shape a distinctive generation of British sports cars.

Mr Forter had seen a rather trendy coupé exhibited at the 1962 Earl's Court Motor Show styled by industrial designer David Ogle. This was the Ogle Mini SX1000 and Forter, something of a

Cosmetics tycoon Boris Forter at the wheel of his Ogle SX-250, based on the ugly Daimler SP250's chassis but – with its ultra-chic looks – one of the most handsome cars on London's streets in 1962.

The Ogle Daimler takes shape in Ogle's Letchworth workshops in 1962: there was just nothing else like it on sale, although Ogle also offered a trendy Mini-based GT coupé.

MAD for it! Imagine it is 1962 and imagine that you set eyes on the SX-250 for the first time. You would probably think it had just arrived from Italy, gleaming away in its champagne paintwork and with its vivid mauve interior. But it was all-British, and a testament to the country's ability to produce excellent car designs.

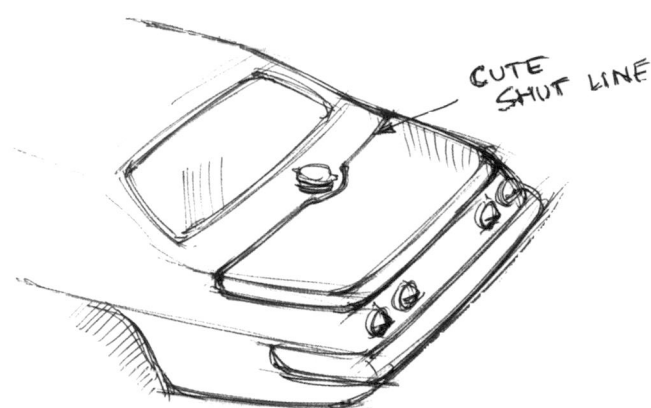

Sketches by Ogle Design's Tom Karen show clever details of the SX-250, including the neat shutline for the boot lid.

Ogle later came up with the Triplex GTS, a glass-topped car based on the SX-250, that was a precursor of the mould-breaking Reliant Scimitar GTE . . . and was also the personal transport for many years of Prince Philip.

car lover, decided Ogle was the man to create his personal set of dream wheels. The resulting Ogle SX-250 sat on a Daimler SP250 chassis, with 2.5-litre V8 engine, and featured glassfibre bodywork like the Ogle Mini. Not only that, it was one of the swishest looking new cars around in 1962 – and also totally unique.

The interior was finished in a colour that had been specially created for Ms Rubinstein's Knightsbridge flat, 'French Violet', while the bodywork was painted in 'Opalescent Golden Sand'. Other features included a special sunroof, reclining seats and thick carpets.

Forter was so delighted that Ogle Design got a lucrative contract to tackle packaging of seven Rubinstein products, and a second Ogle SX-250 was also commissioned. But the car's real significance was that its chic appearance brought it to the attention of Reliant; the three-wheeler maker eventually bought the rights to the car's design and in 1964 launched it with Ford power as the first Reliant Scimitar. The rest, as they say, is history.

SAD for it! It took the savvy of a cosmetics executive to alert the British motor industry to the merits of good-looking cars – and the standard Daimler SP250 could never be called handsome. Seeing his dream car on sale as the Scimitar must have given Boris a wry grin.

With a few styling tweaks, a new chassis and Ford V6 power, the SX-250 was transformed into a production car as the very first Reliant Scimitar.

MOST ATTRACTIVE

OUT OF 10

8th

Built: 1936–40 in Paris, France
Engine: four-cylinder, 1991/2148cc
Top speed: unknown
Sold in the UK? Yes
Number made: 67,840 (all 402 models)

HOW PEUGEOT REDEFINED THE CONVERTIBLE AS TOTALLY ROOFLESS

Renaults and Citroëns were assembled in Britain during the 1930s, and so were familiar sights on our roads. Peugeots, however, were neither. Family-owned Peugeot was founded on making such prosaic items as pepper mills and bicycles, and was among the world's first to manufacture cars in 1889. From being an innovator then, its cars became a bit staid, although robust and reliable, by the mid-1930s. But the 402 changed all that.

The electrically operated roof of the rare Peugeot 402 convertible in action, bringing a bit of motoring theatre to the roads of France in the late 1930s.

The standard 402 was a handsome car even in its standard saloon form. It was designed with aerodynamics in mind, and was inspired by contemporary streamlined American cars like the Chrysler Airflow.

Out went frumpy, square-rigged coachwork and in came one of the most aerodynamic saloon cars then made in Europe – a dead ringer for America's ground-breaking Chrysler Airflow. You could tell it a mile off because its headlights were set close together and positioned, like the car's battery, behind its curved radiator grille.

Underneath, however, things weren't quite so exciting. The four-cylinder 1.9-litre engine developed just 55bhp and, although there was a novel dashboard-mounted gearlever, the promised automatic transmission was never offered.

This wild, be-finned machine is the Peugeot 802, a V8 supercar designed by engineer Jean Andreau; with its V8 engine, it was meant as an export to the USA, but remained a tantalising one-off.

MAD for it!

The Peugeot 402's stunning aerodynamic looks were brilliantly complemented by this high-tech innovation in open-top motoring, creating one of the seminal car designs of the late 1930s. What a wonderful way to cruise through the French countryside – come rain or shine.

However, one truly pace-setting 402 was the convertible. Peugeot had introduced its first power-top open car in 1934. but the 1936 402 *decapotable* was something else, its curvaceous roof packing itself away neatly inside the contours of the equally shapely, rear-hinged boot at the touch of a Bakelite button.

In France at the time, though, this was an expensive plaything. It took Ford's cumbersome Fairlane Sunliner convertible over two decades later to perfect the retractable roof as a production feature. And today's Mercedes-Benz SLK to really make it desirable.

CLEVEREST FEATURES

OUT OF 10

9th

SAD for it!

Well, it looks great with roof up or down, but there's no luggage room in that tapering rear end, the car was no doubt heavy and underpowered, and just imagine those 1930s electrics: if one of the myriad electric motors broke down with the theatrical roof motion in mid-flow, you'd look daft, and probably drenched as well.

The Mercedes-Benz SLK wasn't the first production car in the world with a folding metal top, but it was certainly the first to offer a system that could be easily and reliably used by its owners.

MAD SUPERCARS

It can't have escaped anyone's notice that the modern motoring world is governed, strait-jacketed even, by speed limits. And no matter how much the libertarians protest, these limits are becoming ever more stringent. Only in Germany can you drive your car unfettered, on certain autobahns, at any crazy speed you fancy; bust the speed limit in Britain and you may face a hefty fine; do it in America and you could find yourself forced to attend anger-management classes to expunge those anti-social habits. Even uncongested suburban roads are becoming a jungle of traffic-calming paraphernalia, all of it designed to force you to kill your speed.

All of which makes the very existence of supercars in the twenty-first century something of an anathema. No-one needs a road car that can cruise at over 150mph, do they? Still, major corporations like Volkswagen continue to see a healthy and profitable market for super-fast two-seaters which can almost nudge 200mph while still flattering the massive egos of their owners. The company that brought you the original 'people's car', the Volkswagen Beetle, is now looking to future gold from an outrageous sports car with a 600bhp W12 engine. As a way of opening fat wallets in advance, VW

MOST WEDGE-SHAPED

OUT OF 10

4th

The Ikenga – in the Kikuyu language, it means 'man's life force' – and its designer David Gittens, a graduate of the New York School of Visual Art, October 1968. It was based on a McLaren Can-Am racing chassis with a Chevrolet Camaro V8 engine, and 30,000 people flocked to see it when it was exhibited at Harrods' store.

This horror is the 'Gold Label Powered by Bentley Turbo', a crazy cocktail of cut-and-shut convertible (the body is based on something American, but exactly what I can't tell) and turbocharged Bentley V8 motive power. It was a one-off designed by Robert Jankel, but who knows what the point of it was. . . .

MOST SURPRISING

OUT OF 10

9th

has already proved the car can achieve insane speeds by breaking the 24-hour record at Italy's Nardo test track and achieving an average of 183.45mph.

But will the W12 ever actually go on sale? Supercars, always popular with dreamers, pools-winners and school-boys, rely for their success on booming economic conditions. We don't exactly have those at the moment. A decade ago there was a hopeful outlook for the Yamaha OX-99 and the Bugatti EB110S, both of them outrageous in their own ways. The Yamaha, first revealed in 1992, pre-dated the McLaren F1 in having a central driving position, just like

With its single, centrally mounted driving seat, V8 engine and racing-car inspired dynamics, the Yamaha OX-99 of 1992 promised to be the ultimate in rich men's playthings for the road. Unfortunately, potential buyers vanished like a puff of exhaust smoke as recession bit.

This is the dramatic Volkswagen W12 roadster, revealed in 1998 and now proven as an astonishing performer; a coupé version circled Italy's Nardo track for twenty-four hours and averaged just under 184mph. And there are plans to offer the car for sale to the public – it's all a long way from the VW Beetle.

The Bugatti EB110S was, for a very short time, officially the fastest road car on the planet, and the Italian company even managed to sell 139 cars, including one to Michael Schumacher, before its position became unsustainable in the face of an economic downturn, and it went into receivership.

The single-seater Illusion took designer Dave Puhl three years to build, had a Ford V8 engine, and a V-shaped handlebar in place of a steering wheel. Its moment of glory, however, was to promote Petersen Publishing at the 1966 New York Automobile Show, here aided by Brigitte Eichenauer, a former Miss Frankfurt.

a Grand Prix racing car. Its design, including its 3.5-litre V12 engine and hyper-aerodynamic body, was conceived and created in the UK, but despite much excitement from car fanatics, Yamaha wisely decided that the outlook was not optimistic enough to actually make the car.

Bugatti did get a stage further, opening a factory in Modena in Italy in

DAFTEST FEATURES OUT OF 10 10th

The six-wheeled Wolfrace Sonic was intended to advertise the wheel company's products, like the ones fitted to the Ford Capri 2.8i and MG Metro. Here, though, it's promoting a long-forgotten pop record in 1981 by one Wolfie Witcher – that's him with the spanner.

1991, and producing 139 of the mid-engined EB110 and its S sibling. Briefly the fastest production car on the planet, and numbering Michael Schumacher among its intrigued owners, the revived Bugatti enterprise eventually went pear-shaped, and the receivers could interest no-one in the project. Those wily folk at Volkswagen acquired the brand name, but even this industrial giant is hesitating to market a brand-new Bugatti. Perhaps it is altogether safer just to create supercars on an individual basis – create an exciting and dramatic vehicle, and use it to promote something else. The Illusion you see on these pages was, indeed, used primarily to promote a motor show, and the 1982 Wolfrace Sonic was a mobile advertisement for alloy wheels. In an intriguing joint-venture, film director Steven Spielberg

Steven Spielberg is a devoted Lexus owner, so for his recent futuristic flick *Minority Report* he called in the Japanese luxury car division of Toyota to help him create a supercar of the future. Technical details are, as you can guess, pretty sketchy, but then again, your grandson could actually own a Lexus Movie one day.

CLEVEREST FEATURES OUT OF 10 4th

The Cizeta Moroder V16T was a short-lived attempt to revive interest in a V16-powered car – something not seen since the 1930s. The Italian brutes were handmade and, allegedly, extremely fast and powerful, but only about a dozen were built, starting in 1988, before Giorgio Moroder's vanity project disappeared.

MOST
ATTRACTIVE

OUT OF 10

4th

Karmann took an iconic Mercedes-Benz feature of the past – gullwing doors – and added it to a Mercedes-Benz of the present (1993) to create a hybrid 300SL with showmanship aplenty. You could never actually buy one, of course, but Karmann gained enough column inches to make the enterprise worthwhile.

MOST
WEDGE-SHAPED

OUT OF 10

1st

The 1980 Aston Martin Bulldog was certainly dramatic, fulfilling its brief as a corporate attention-getter in one of Aston's periodic 'difficult' eras. With its mid-mounted V8 engine and dramatic wedge profile, it had the right ingredients. But those gullwing doors were a pain, drenching occupants as they opened them on wet days.

has teamed up with Lexus to produce a supercar of the future. It's called the Lexus Movie, and is a star of Spielberg's latest blockbuster, *Minority Report*. Both Lexus's designers and Spielberg's special effects people collaborated on this dramatic supercar, albeit one that cannot reach its awesome claimed top speed without computer-generated effects. To car buyers it promotes the film, and to filmgoers it promotes Lexus.

The worlds of cars and entertainment collided in 1988. This was the year when Italian engineer Claudio Zampolli teamed up with record producer Giorgio Moroder to give a wide-eyed public the Cizeta Moroder V16, the first V16-engined car since the Cadillac V16 of 1930s. This wondrous object, which could out-Lamborghini a Lamborghini, was allegedly able to hit a ridiculously high speed with neck-straining acceleration, and a tiny handful – perhaps no more than a dozen – were produced before the good sense intrinsic to not losing vast fortunes kicked in.

Exactly fifty years ago the car on everyone's lips was the Mercedes-Benz 300SL, the first production car with fuel-injection and gullwing doors, and an easy victor at Le Mans and on the Carrera PanAmericana races. Those incredible doors have rarely been seen in production since, with the exception of the ill-fated De Loran DMC-12 of 1979. German coachbuilder Karmann revived the feature for a modified version of the contemporary Mercedes-Benz SL in 1993, which looked completely normal

with the gullwing doors closed and sensational with them open. In 1980 Britain's own Aston Martin also incorporated gullwing doors on the dramatic Bulldog, an extraordinary wedge-shaped supercar; in this case, the gullwing doors were not such a success, as the driver and passenger were apt to become drenched when exiting the Bulldog on a wet day. Still, both of these cars were really created to act as honeypots to the

bees of the car industry, who would be encouraged to employ Karmann and Aston Martin's engineering division Tickford on lucrative projects.

In a similar vein, Italdesign has been a regular touter for trade with a dizzying array of supercar concepts. While the company has churned out designs for family cars such as the Fiat Panda and Volkswagen Golf, its showcases, such as the Maserati-based Boomerang of 1972 –

This is the 1972 Maserati Boomerang, one of a large number of concept cars from the studios of Italdesign and its founder Giorgetto Giugiaro. As you can imagine, it proved just too radical to interest Maserati in a production version, but the lone prototype lives on in the hands of a German owner who loves it to bits.

to name but one from an enormous list – have remained mildly interesting sideshows in the fairground of car design, mostly judged simply too mad to actually make.

THE 'MOSCHINO'
ROVER METRO IN
DETAIL

Built: 1995 in
Longbridge, Birmingham
Engine: four-cylinder,
1396cc
Top speed: 104mph
Sold in the UK? No
Number made: 1

CHARMS, CHARITIES AND THE MOST FASHIONABLE METRO EVER

*C*ars take too long to design to succumb to fashion; they're too expensive to develop to be fripperies. Which tends to mean their colours and interior trim err on the side of universal and sober acceptability. Hence the straightforward reds, blues, silvers and whites, mostly with grey trim, we all put up with.

In 1995, however, the Italian fashion industry set out to prove not all small cars need look standard-issue. At the Turin motor show, Italy's world renowned couture houses showed us how.

Moschino's fashion-conscious Rover Metro in all its over-the-top glory, something to put curses on and bring good luck to other road users in about equal measure.

DAFTEST
FEATURES

OUT OF 10

8th

The standard Rover Metro, in this case a 1.4GTA, certainly looked a bit naked by comparison with the Moschino creation, if a tiny bit more subtle.

On this 'carwalk', Gucci stuck red and green stripes down the side of a Cinquecento, Fendi added their trademark gold and brown parallel lines to a Suzuki Swift, Krizia kitted a Golf estate out with snakeskin-pattern leather, and Missoni swapped Lancia badges on a Y10 for its own.

Moschino, though, did its bit for Britain by decorating a white Metro in black and lucky symbols – cats, horseshoes and number 13s. Inside were black-and-white striped seat covers with red edging.

The cars were all auctioned after the show, with proceeds going to AIDS research, so somewhere in Italy, although it looks like a Metro that's been attacked by a graffiti gang, someone is pounding the streets in a Moschino designer original. Perhaps grey with black seats isn't so bad after all.

 MAD for it! Fashion designers have a bigger influence on cars than you might think – Missoni created the interior of the Maserati Biturbo, for instance, and Jasper Conran has issued a limited-edition Mazda MX-5 – but few cars have been as ostentatiously 'designer' as this charity-boosting little number.

New styling, engines and suspension transformed the Metro in 1990 from a humble runabout favoured by the motoring feeble to a peppy little hot hatchback; this is a 1.4GTi 16V.

 SAD for it! Hmm, well, compared to some of Rover's own limited edition Metros over the years, this one has a touch of class, I suppose. You'd look like a mad witch or a fortune-teller driving it down the high street, but in this Harry Potter-obsessed world, that might be no bad thing. . . .

One thing Moschino did was brighten up the interior: the standard issue, even in the sporty 1.4GTi 16V as here, was pretty awful – Midlands grey plastic and naff upholstery at its typical worst.

THE SAAB SONETT IN DETAIL

Built: 1966-72 in Linkoping, Sweden
Engine: three-cylinder, 841cc and V4, 1498cc
Top speed: 100mph
Sold in the UK? No
Number made: 10,219

MOST SURPRISING

OUT OF 10

6th

SPORTY SWEDE? BJORN BORG IS PROBABLY MORE ENTERTAINING

Bet you never knew Saab sold over 10,000 sports cars between 1966 and 1974. As a British car-spotter, your ignorance is understandable: none were officially sold here and the vast majority built were shipped from Sweden straight to the USA.

Saab first toyed with building a two-seater in 1956 with the Sonett I, a dainty roadster with a novel aluminium box-section chassis and plastic body. It was intended as a pure competition car but, when rallying rules relaxed, Saab's beetle-backed saloons were just as eligible, and the Sonett was abandoned. Six were made and five survive.

This nifty little number was Saab's first-ever sports car. But despite its aluminium box-section chassis, glassfibre body and peppy performance, the 1956 Sonett roadster never made it to production.

This stylish coupé was the first on-sale Sonett in 1966, a low-slung two-seater initially offered with Saab's two-stroke engine and an instant hit. Anyone who drove one immediately liked it.

MAD for it! Saabs have always been curiously attractive, and the Swedish take on the sports car theme was no exception. Great to drive with excellent handling, and mostly quite good-looking too, they helped put the marque on the map in the USA. It's a shame they weren't replaced.

In 1963, though, the sporty Saab concept was revived and the result was the Sonett II of 1966, a waist-high two-seat coupé. The first 258 ran Saab's venerable two-stroke three-cylinder engine, but thereafter the Sonett used a 1.5-litre Ford V4 motor and sales, especially in America, snowballed.

Saab couldn't leave well alone, though. The car was restyled twice, latterly in Italy, and ended up looking none-too-pretty with its oversize, impact-absorbing bumpers and tapir-like nose.

The first production Sonett boasted an amazingly slender drag co-efficient of 0.32; the last possessed the somewhat less dramatic novelty of headlamp wipers.

Sadly, in the 1970s fuel crises the Sonett was not replaced. A crying shame because it was speedy and a delight to drive.

A major re-design took away the Sonett's daintiness and replaced it with typically Swedish love-it-or-hate-it styling. Still, the by-now standard Ford V4 gave the little car plenty of poke.

SAD for it! Saab makes sensible and safe - very safe - cars for architects and photographers, and its dalliance with the world of sports cars was a slightly crazy aberration. Weedy engines and, in the end, pretty odd styling meant they were not replaced.

Just to spoil the Sonett even further, Saab was obliged to fit cumbersome, energy-absorbing bumpers to it to ensure it met crash regulations in what became its biggest market – the USA.

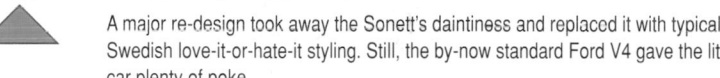

Built: 1965–67 in
Prestwick, Ayrshire,
Scotland (Scamp) and
1971–78 in Tullos,
Aberdeen, Scotland
(Parabug)

Engine: electric motor
(Scamp), four-cylinder,
1131/1192/1285/1493/
1584cc (Parabug)

Top speed: 36mph
(Scamp), 70mph approx.
(Parabug)

Sold in the UK? Yes
(Scamp), Yes (Parabug)

Number made: 12
(Scamp), unknown
(Parabug)

NORTH-OF-THE-BORDER DUO FAILED TO PUT SCOTLAND ON THE CAR MAP

Scots are responsible for some of the greatest of engineering feats but, curiously, their country's made little impact on the car world. Nevertheless, a permanent shrine to Scotland's cars exists in the former home of one of its pioneer marques, Argyll. The company's magnificent factory beside Loch Lomond opened in 1906 and now, as well as housing a factory-outlet shopping centre, boasts the Scottish Motor Heritage Centre.

An Argyll, probably an Angus Sanderson and an Arrol Johnston are sure to be on display. You can bank on a Scottish-made Hillman Imp too. But there won't be a Scamp or a Parabug because the Heritage Centre couldn't find one of either. Not surprising, really: both are like hens' teeth.

There was plenty of interest in the Scamp at the Ideal Home Exhibition as the perfect electric runabout for shopping and local errands. Sadly the car was to prove anything but robust when it was actually driven on the road.

MOST USELESS

OUT OF 10

7th

Scamp & Parabug

The Scamp was an abortive attempt by Scottish Aviation of Prestwick to design an electric shopping car. The 1965 prototype, with 36mph top speed and 30-mile range, was so promising the Electricity Board offered to sell the cars through its 2,000 UK showrooms. It was even shown at the 1967 Ideal Home Exhibition.

However, the lack of batteries that would last beyond twelve months, and the fact that the suspension collapsed during tests at MIRA – the Scamp had minuscule 8in wheels – meant the project was abandoned after just twelve had been made.

No better luck befell the Parabug. Devised by Glasgow industrial designers Anderson Bonar and built in Aberdeen by a plastics moulding company, the Parabug was a kit to transform an elderly Volkswagen Beetle into a stark, straight-lined off-roader like a Mini Moke.

Despite a brochure that quoted J.R.R. Tolkien's *The Hobbit* ('Roads go ever on, over rock and under tree . . .') and a starting price for the kit of just £165, very few were sold.

If you know the whereabouts of examples of either, the Scottish Motor Heritage Centre needs to hear from you.

Here is a Parabug in action, manfully splashing through a puddle. The designer was clearly a right-angle fanatic, but you could build a Parabug using any forlorn old VW Beetle, plus a bit of spannering savvy.

MAD for it! What is it with the Scots? They have an excellent engineering heritage and they come up with interesting car designs like the thrifty, manoeuvrable Scamp and the go-anywhere Parabug, but have proved themselves incapable of sustaining an indigenous car industry. Which is a pity.

SAD for it! What is it with the Scots? They have an excellent engineering heritage and yet they come up with crackers car designs like the brittle, useless Scamp and the lash-up Parabug, proving themselves completely incapable of sustaining an indigenous car industry. Which is a relief.

Built: 1953 in Coventry, West Midlands
Engine: four-cylinder, 1497cc
Top speed: 75mph approx.
Sold in the UK? Yes
Number made: 6 approx.

PLASTIC WAS DRASTIC BUT SINGER HAD COME TO THE END OF THE ROAD

The world's first production car with a plastic body was the 1953 Chevrolet Corvette, a glassfibre classic, while Britain's Jensen 541 soon followed. Both were successes. Which is more than can be said for this dumpy little convertible. It's a Singer, and it could have beaten the Jensen to the showrooms if its maker hadn't been in such a sorry state at the time it was revealed – October 1953.

MAD for it!

This little four-seater roadster could have been a winner for Singer, with its neat design and lightweight plastic bodywork. The company had a good reputation, especially abroad, and its glassfibre experience was well ahead of its rivals. If only the cash hadn't run out at just the wrong time.

'Singer Export' gives you an idea of what the ailing company had in mind for its innovative plastic-bodied tourer – could it ever have been a hit in far-flung places?

The upright and slab-sided Singer SM1500, with which the SMX shared many parts, was a decent enough car, but neither nimble nor attractive enough to set it apart from rivals made by larger companies.

SAD for it! Not long after this bizarre mixture of the ancient and the futuristic came along, Citroen launched its DS and Fiat its 600 – truly the cars of the future. Singer's pathetic last gasps were misguided and weird, and it was left to the energetic Rootes Group to rescue something from this floundering malaise.

When Singer lost its independence to the Rootes Group this was the result: the 1956 Gazelle was really just a Hillman Minx with Singer's twin-cam engine and even this terrific power unit was dropped after two years.

The 1946 model Singer Roadster was typical of the rugged, spritely and thrifty little cars that endeared the marque to so many customers; modern, however, it certainly was not.

The 'Export' number plate and left-hand drive hint at the SMX's intended destiny. Singer Motors hoped the easily mouldable four-seater tourer would be a hit in the kind of balmy colonial markets which had, for years, been happily lapping up its Olde English models. Indeed, the previous model, the 1951–53 4AD Roadster, had been for export only.

Alas, even though the car was one of the most keenly viewed new models at the Earl's Court motor show (the *Daily Express* hailed it as 'the car of the future'), Singer was virtually bankrupt, having spent a fortune developing its slow-selling SM1500 and Hunter saloons while operating in a positively archaic multi-storey Coventry factory.

Just as the SMX should have been rolling on to the quay in Malaysia and Uruguay in 1954, Singer was snapped up by the Rootes Group. From then until 1969, when the name was discontinued, Singers were merely re-labelled Hillman Minxes.

Singer's plastic adventures were not all in vain; a handful of Hunter saloons boasted plastic bonnets and boot lids. Probably only half a dozen SMXs were made and one at least still exists.

MAD THREE-WHEELERS

MAD THREE-WHEELERS

Caught off-balance: the concept that neve seems to work

You will, I am sure, be familiar with the often-repeated assertion that a stool with three legs is inherently more stable than a stool with four legs. There must somewhere be a complicated geometric diagram which can prove this. But a three-legged stool never feels particularly stable, does it?

In exactly the same way, there has long been a school of thought in the car world that three-wheelers offer a number of advantages over their four-square counterparts. These benefits include more agile handling, lower running costs and in many cases even tax advantages. In the UK you can drive a three-wheeler – classified by law as a tricycle – on a motorbike driving licence, as long as the vehicle weighs less than 500kg.

Think of three-wheelers in a British context and I am pretty certain that your mind will be filled with the products of the Reliant Motor Company, a sixty-seven-year-old institution.

Its pint-sized family cars, the Regal, Robin and Rialto, can hardly be judged as unsuccessful, and their thousands of enthusiastic owners would certainly not consider their vehicles at all mad. The Reliant TW9, however, is a bit on the bonkers side: with a passenger cab that has a strange, insect-like quality to it, the TW9 was intended to be the commercial vehicle of choice for the

For many globe-trotters, the whole concept of three-wheelers is redolent of cheap taxi rides on Indian or Far Eastern travels. Most of them look more flimsy than this intriguing four-door saloon, the Italindo Super Helicak built in Jakarta, Indonesia – a vehicle that you trust your driver will pilot with extreme care when you're on board. . . .

This bug-eyed device is a street-sweeper based on the Reliant TW9, a combination pitched straight at fiscally prudent local councils and other, smaller businesses. However, despite its manoeuvrability and economy, the TW9 was strangely shunned by most of British industry.

MOST USELESS
OUT OF 10
3rd

MOST WEDGE-SHAPED
OUT OF 10
3rd

And for those reading this book in black-and-white, this is the Bond Bug in the only colour available, light grey – I mean, bright orange. 'Driver girls and passenger girls', reads the caption, 'they all fall for the speedy, top economy Bond Bug'. Which wasn't strictly true: fewer than 3,000 were sold in four years.

small business or financially prudent local authority, having a chassis that could be adopted to any number of applications. Launched in 1967, only 1,888 were sold over twenty years, which sounds mildly impressive until you realise Ford shifted that number of Escort vans per month. Reliant had little more success in trying to interest the young and hip in the three-wheeled concept. The racy 1970 Bond Bug was a

radical interpretation of the theme. It came only in bright orange, had a lift-up canopy instead of doors, and looked for all the world like a wedge on wheels. It was pitched at the trendy kid-about-town, yet only 2,770 were sold over four years.

That a three-wheeler could be successful was amply proved by no less a company than BMW in the 1950s. Starting in 1953, it built under licence a version of the Italian Isetta bubble car for the German market, as a way of staving off bankruptcy. The curvy little car proved

MOST
SURPRISING

OUT OF 10

3rd

BMW
Isetta

MOST
WEDGE-SHAPED

OUT OF 10

8th

MOST
USELESS

OUT OF 10

8th

The Isetta typified the 1950s bubble car breed in the days before the Fiat 500 or Mini. The tiny, egg-shaped car, with its entire front doubling as the only door, originated in Italy but BMW manufactured it under licence, and the Isetta provided much of the financial foundations that underpin BMW today.

a good seller for the company, providing the finance which turned it into today's maker of executive expresses. Clive Sinclair, however, did not see such prosperity from his foray into the world of three-wheeled transport. With the success of his digital watches, calculators and computers bolstering his confidence, he launched the ill-starred Sinclair C5 trike in 1985. This single seater electric runabout, originally intended as a way for children to get themselves to school on the pavement, was a classic and now iconic business failure, pilloried by the tabloids and shunned by serious motorists.

The truth is that major car manufacturers have avoided the three-wheeled vehicle like the plague. Sure, every now and again there has been a toe in the water: Ford's Ghia Cockpit, a motor show concept car of 1983, at least proved it was possible to make a three-wheeler stylish, but the fact that such a car never came anywhere near reaching the showrooms should tell you all you need to know about the lack of credibility that cars on three wheels enjoy.

One three-wheeler that needs no introduction is the Sinclair C5, launched in 1985 and instantly ridiculed by the press, as well as being slammed on safety grounds. Which was all a bit unfair: it had originally been conceived as a fun way for kids to get to school – on the pavement.

The mainstream motor industry has long given the whole concept of three-wheeled vehicles an extremely wide berth, but occasionally designers have a crack at it. This is Ford's Ghia Cockpit of 1981, said to give the feeling of being in a fighter plane . . . while still returning 75mpg from a single-cylinder engine mounted inside the back wheel. Cool.

'Mummy, when are we going to get a proper car?' The rudimentary charm of many British three-wheelers, like this rare Powerdrive dating from 1958, was all right while the country was still on a semi-war footing, but the Mini couldn't come a day too soon for those embarrassed at school home time.

Yet this has not put off scores of attempts to design and market winning three-wheelers. Starting in the 1950s there were several British attempts, one of the neatest of which was the Powerdrive, which at least had the single wheel at the back and possessed some semblance of normality at the front. Most of these cars were rendered redundant by the introduction of, first, the Fiat 500 in 1957 and then, two years later, the Mini. But some people never give up. Alan Hatswell thought he would have a go in the 1980s, with his tiny three-wheeled Cursor, a distinctly dangerous-looking device with a 49cc moped engine tucked away in its pointed tail. He managed to sell around fifty of these starting in 1985 before, like many before him, giving up.

And then there was the Danish Mini-El City, a three-wheeler that mixed a vaguely C5-like shape with the lift-up

These days a cursor is that maddeningly sensitive little thing that darts all over your computer screen. In 1985 a Cursor was a maddeningly sensitive little thing that darted all over the road, spluttering along on its 49cc moped engine and looking like it had been knocked up in someone's shed. Still, they sold a few.

There was a legal rumpus over the name of this Danish electric commuter car after Rover objected to it being called the Mini-El City. It's shown here in the Imperial Gardens in Cheltenham in 1992. While it was fairly successful in urban parts of the Netherlands, it failed to catch on in the UK.

canopy of the Bond Bug and electric power. It was quite a neat idea but, as usual, why would you accept a wheel less when it comes to being out on busy roads?

Some have gone a stage further, and come up with a two-wheeled car. That was what the Monotrace purported to be although, with 'stabiliser' wheels either side of its narrow tandem two-seater body to stop it tipping over at traffic lights, it was hardly a claim that stands up. It was typical of the sort of contraption earnest French manufacturers knocked out before the Second World War – if there was a new motoring fad in the offing, they wanted a part of it. The Monotrace was made between 1926 and 1930 in Saint Etienne, Loire, but it was too Heath Robinson-esque even for France. Its single-cylinder, 510cc engine was concealed in its tail, driving the rear wheel via chains through a motorbike gearbox, while the driver, sitting behind the most meagre of windscreens, steered using a giant pair of handlebars. The inspiration for the design actually came from Germany, where it was devised in 1923 by the Mauser armaments factory as the Einsperauto – a single-track 'car'.

With, it appears, Harry Enfield's Mr Cholmondeley-Warner at the, er, handlebars, this two-wheeled Monotrace is all set for action. Question is, how did this weird French contraption come to be outside the Bangor Hotel, somewhere in England, in I believe the 1940s? Answers on a postcard, please.

DAFTEST FEATURES

OUT OF 10

6th

THE SKODA FELICIA IN DETAIL

Built: 1958–64 in Mlada Boleslav, former Czechoslovakia

Engine: four-cylinder, 1089/1221cc

Top speed: 81mph

Sold in the UK? Yes

Number made: 15,864

BEHIND THE IRON CURTAIN IN THE 1950s, THIS WAS THE AUDI TT OF ITS TIME

Skoda celebrated its 100th birthday in 1995 at the same time as launching a massively improved version of its Favorit hatchback, and reviving the Felicia name for it. Just as the Favorit evoked a long-forgotten Skoda of the 1930s, so the Felicia revived a name last used by the Czech car maker in 1964.

You can't look at the Felicia and not be charmed by the convertible Skoda's collection of characteristically 1950s features, especially the little tailfins and streamlined bulges over the front wheels.

Skoda today refers to the old Felicia with all the affection and reverence that Jaguar might use for the E-type or Porsche the 356. Was it really much cop?

Frankly, probably not. When introduced in 1958, the two-seater convertible Felicia was neither especially handsome nor particularly rapid, twin carburettors notwithstanding.

Its archaic separate chassis, swing axle rear suspension and tall, skinny wheels also meant it could be a treacherous handful on rain-soaked roads.

MOST ATTRACTIVE
OUT OF 10
5th

The Felicia has an appealingly pugnacious look at the front; but take a corner too fast in the wet and the styling will be the last thing on your mind as you battle to control the car's wayward handling.

But what it did possess was a healthy appetite for tough and long service and the sort of pugnacious, comradely charm now utterly squeezed out of Skoda by parent corporation Volkswagen.

The old Felicia, with some 16,000 made and a handful sold in England, stuck out like a sore thumb from its contemporaries. Today's Fabia, competent vehicle though it is, certainly doesn't. With rose-tinted headlights, maybe that's exactly what Skoda wants.

MAD for it! A tough and simple convertible with charmingly 1950s lines, the Felicia was from the days before Skoda went awry and tried to do a VW Beetle on the cheap. Owners rate the car as pretty good, and it makes a splendid period piece in the face of today's motoring uniformity.

It was an unlikely candidate for revival, the Felicia name, but it popped up again on the thoroughly revised version of the Skoda Favorit in 1994 as Volkswagen gave the formerly Czech marque a new lease of life.

SAD for it! The Felicia wasn't as rubbish as later Skodas but, by the standards of 1958, it was still pretty rubbish, with its old-fashioned separate chassis and appalling handling. For the unfortunate Czech driver of the time, though, the only alternative was the Skoda Octavia, a Felicia with a roof, so for many it was a Skoda or walking (there has to be a joke in there somewhere, doesn't there?).

A neat glassfibre hardtop transformed the open Felicia into a snug and snow-proof little coupé for those bitterly cold Eastern Bloc winters of the early 1960s.

THE STEYR-PUCH
HAFLINGER IN DETAIL

Built: 1959–74 in Graz,
Austria
Engine: two-cylinder,
700cc
Top speed: 50mph
Sold in the UK? Yes
Number made: 19,564
approx

MUD-SLINGING HAFLINGER MADE LIGHT OF AN UPHILL STRUGGLE

The British Army is increasingly ordering an impressive six-wheel drive off-roader called a Pinzgauer as a replacement for its old Land-Rover ambulances. It used to be made in Austria by Steyr-Daimler-Puch, a little-known company in the UK but one that makes components for 40 per cent of the world's four-wheel drive cars. Now the plant that makes it has relocated to Guildford in Surrey, to be closer to that important customer in Aldershot.

And its pint-size ancestor, the Haflinger, also came to Britain in the 1960s and early '70s where it sold in small numbers to farmers with a technological bent.

The Haflinger was a tiny and ingeniously simple 4x4 utility vehicle with a 40bhp 700cc air-cooled twin-cylinder engine at the back, differential locks at front and rear, and all-independent suspension.

MOST USEFUL

OUT OF 10

7th

A Haflinger at its happiest, clattering up Austrian mountainsides to get its driver to places even your average goat-herd would find just a mite inaccessible.

Brand new Haflingers get the sign-off at Steyr-Puch's factory in Graz in 1967 – in fifty years almost 20,000 were sold across Europe, including in Britain.

In appearance, the Haflinger was starkly industrial, with its basic pressed steel structure and canvas top. In action, it was nothing short of incredible, clattering its way up 50 degree slopes with gusto and scattering mud as it bounced across soggy farmland.

Far too utilitarian for today's 4x4 buyers, almost 20,000 were made from 1959 until 1974. Most that came to Britain are probably still going strong although, like the Mini Moke, the used Haflinger was a Bohemian favourite in the 1970s. A British owners' club exists for survivors.

Haflinger components are assembled in a spotlessly clean Steyr workshop in the 1960s. The engine also found its way into Steyr's 650TR, an Austrian-built version of the Fiat 500.

MAD for it! The perfect mechanical companion for hill farmers throughout Europe, there was simply nothing like the Haflinger in its 1960s heyday. Incredible to think that this pint-sized mudplugger led directly to the Pinzgauer that is keeping the British Army on patrol from Bovingdon to Bosnia.

SAD for it! There aren't many of these bouncy little Haflingers left – most working people who used to find them invaluable have moved on to quadbikes, which are cheaper to run and just as practical, or else the four-wheel drive Suzuki Jimny and Subaru Justy, which are a bit more user-friendly.

The Fiat Panda 4x4 was a combination of everything Graz had worked on, a Fiat-based 4x4 economy car that could double as a versatile and sure-footed runabout in rural mud or holiday snow.

THE TRIUMPH SILVER BULLET IN DETAIL

Built: 1950 in Coventry, West Midlands
Engine: four-cylinder, 2088cc
Top speed: 90mph
Sold in the UK? No
Number made: 3

WITH A CLICK AND A WHIRR, THE SILVER BULLET WENT UP IN FLAMES

Remember the 'sit-up-and-beg' convertible that TV's Channel Islands detective *Bergerac* drove – a Triumph Roadster? The Silver Bullet was the all-British glamour wagon intended to replace it. Announced in 1950, the Bullet, also known as the TR-X, boasted torpedo-like bodywork with enclosed rear wheels that was space-age beside the matronly Roadster. The price was announced as £1,246.

MAD for it!

Here was a car Dan Dare could be pleased with, a two-seater sportster positively alive with electric gadgets. Okay, so they didn't always work properly, but every new car has its teething problems. Perhaps, with a little more development time, and maybe fewer toys, this could have been a top-seller.

A launch photo of the Triumph TR-X or Silver Bullet roadster, depending on what you prefer to call it; it might have been stylish but those barrel sides concealed a lethal labyrinth of combustible electrics that ensured the car was rapidly abandoned.

Under this aluminium skin whirred a high-tech hornet's nest of hydraulics: the headlamps popped up electrically, as did the hood, windows, radio aerial and even the bonnet; the overdrive on the three-speed gearbox was also electro-hydraulically driven, and so were the seat adjustment controls.

An electric motor under the bonnet drove the system, which was sand-wiched inside the double-skinned bodywork.

But the Silver Bullet was bedevilled by problems. When it was demonstrated to Princess Margaret none of the buttons matched the right functions, and when a prototype was out roadtesting later an engine fire broke out under the bonnet. This shorted the wiring, the power to open the bonnet was therefore lost, and the un-extinguishable flames roared inside until the car was completely burned out.

After this the Silver Bullet plans were torn up and Triumph turned instead to the simple and altogether less com-bustible TR2 sports car.

You might be familiar with the Triumph Roadster from creaking repeats of TV detective show Bergerac – it was the car the Silver Bullet tried to replace.

SAD for it! The Silver Bullet was a typically half-baked British attempt at a glamorous car tipped at wealthy US customers. In its haste to get its hands on their dollars, Standard/Triumph cobbled together this ill-conceived sports car packed with unreliable electrical connections, with predictably disastrous results.

Another prototype to replace the Triumph Roadster, but this time one destined for greatness, was the 'New Sports Car', revealed at the 1952 Earl's Court motor show. With another re-design the car became the much-loved TR2.

Built: 1978 in Luton,
Bedfordshire
Engine: four-cylinder,
2279cc
Top speed: unknown
Sold in the UK? No
Number made: 1

MOST
WEDGE-SHAPED
OUT OF 10
10th

A SHARP SPORTS CAR BUT IT STILL COULDN'T STEM VAUXHALL'S DECLINE

This is the Equus, Latin for horse, and unlike any Vauxhall you're ever likely to see on the road. For anyone who thinks the Triumph TR7 was wedge-shapedly ugly, then the Equus takes the form to another dimension, with its straight, angular lines and knife-edge profile. The time was 1978 and the Equus then represented the very latest in sports car design. Even so, it's hard to believe this car is now twenty-four years old.

It also has the distinction of being the very last all-British designed Vauxhall, until today's Lotus Elise-based VX220.

The Equus was widely tipped as an up-to-the-minute British successor to the MGB – an affordable sports car for everyone. And grandiose plans were drawn up to make it by Panther, on whose Lima sports car chassis the Equus was based.

No mistaking its boldness, but the Equus attempted to cash in on the pent-up demand for new British sports cars. With the TR7 fading, however, it was obvious the end was in sight for wedge shapes.

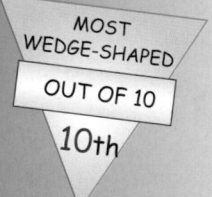

This is the Panther Lima, on whose traditional separate chassis the Equus was based. They also shared the Vauxhall Magnum 2.3-litre engine (although this is actually one of the very rare 1.8 Limas).

MAD for it!

Vauxhall's design department at Luton employed some talented people, including Wayne Cherry, the man responsible for the Equus' sharp lines. Most of their work was on Bedford trucks, which was a shame because the Equus could have been a real hit at the time.

But when Vauxhall's design department shut down in 1980, all Vauxhall development transferred to Opel in Germany, and any hope for such quintessentially British projects as the Equus were dashed. The car remained a one-off styling exercise.

Strangely, although Vauxhall makes much of its heritage, opening a special collection of its heirlooms at Luton a few years ago, the Equus isn't part of it and it barely merits a mention in Vauxhall's official history book.

SAD for it! The TR7 was already something of a joke when the Equus came along, and Vauxhall's design department was soon closed down for a very good reason: the cars they churned out tended to be rather worse than their Opel cousins in Germany.

Looks a bit naff with all that red carpet and grey plastic, but at least Vauxhall was trying to put some verve back into the motoring scene with the Equus, the work of designer Wayne Cherry. ▶

Front view of the Equus helps make its stark lines a bit more palatable. It was revealed in 1978 and for three years Vauxhall pondered making it, before finally consigning the two-seater to its museum. ▼

They thought it was all over, Vauxhall's sports car aspiration, and then in 2000 along came the VX220, a ground-hugging two-seater based on the mid-engined Lotus Elise chassis and, indeed, built by Lotus. Despite rave reviews the car's been a sluggish seller.

MAD TINY CARS

Small things bright and beautiful, plus some that weren't!

Good things, we are taught from an early age, often come in small packages. Is that the case with cars? Well, that is what many would have us believe, and the evidence has never been more plain to see. The popularity of the MCC Smart City Coupé has confounded the critics, who maintained the motoring public would never take to such a small car, one that appears to have lost both its bonnet and its boot in a road rage incident.

The Smart, which went on sale in 1998, is small in every way, from the diameter of its wheels to the size of its luggage compartment, but – crucially – it can accommodate two grown-up urbanites in comfort, and offers spritely performance while costing nothing to run and being parkable, virtually on your doormat. Unlike many previous attempts at a minimal city car, however, the Smart is also desirable, thanks to its general niftiness. You can not only thank Mercedes-Benz for that, but also the Swatch watch company, whose founder Nicholas Hayek came up with the concept in the first place.

If you can rewind your mind half a century, you may recall the explosion in so-called bubble cars in Europe in the early 1950s. Most of these characterful

Two prototypes for the MCC Smart, neither of which are very far from the finished product. Despite pessimistic predictions the Smart, with its tiny size and thirst and natty details, has become a common sight in most big European cities. For its size, the Smart is the most successful car of all time.

but homespun contraptions were made redundant by the introduction, in 1957, of the Fiat 500. The remaining survivors of the breed were wiped out by the Mini two years later. In an even more bygone era, in fact before the First World War, a similar purge was initiated against the flimsy and dangerous open 'cyclecars' of France, after Peugeot introduced a 'real' car in miniature. They called it the Bébé and it was a roaring success.

The lesson seems to be that little cars are fine so long as they are good. It's about the herd mentality. If everyone else is doing it, then I will too. Which, perhaps, helps to explain why bizarre-looking small cars tend to have been failures. Take the Hrubon. Built in France from 1980 to 1988, the Hrubon looked just like a Mini Moke, the quintessential British 1960s fun car, but at half the length. And then there was the Tici, also Mini-powered but hailing from Nottingham in the UK, a minuscule, wedge-shaped roadster that was either entirely daft or utterly dinky depending on your frame of mind. The fact was, though, you would look like a gnome if you drove either of these silly vehicles, and who wants to look like a gnome? The French, apparently.

Despite producing some of the world's favourite economy cars, such as the Renault 4 and Citroën 2CV, there has long been a reasonable market there for microcars, bizarre vehicles that can be driven without a car licence, just as long as their specifications remain within set parameters. These govern engine size,

dimensions and performance. Some have managed to look cute, such as the 1972 William, a sort of bulimic Land Rover from the creators of the Lambretta

The 1957 Fiat Nuova 500 was post-war Europe's first, modern 'real car in miniature' and, at a stroke, it rendered the flotilla of bubble cars and three-wheeled death-traps that had sprung up after the Second World War utterly obsolete. It was on sale until 1972, and is still much loved.

A 1914 Peugeot Bébé: this was one of the first decent small cars to emerge from Europe once the novelty of the motor car had worn off and manufacturers realised they were in the consumer products business, and needed to come up with cars boasting the widest possible appeal.

scooter. Others have had motorsport credibility, like the Ligier series from the fertile mind of Formula One team owner Guy Ligier. And yet more, and there are many more, are just plain sad, like the hideous Riboud you see here – an uncomfortable mix of golf cart and shopping trolley.

Major car manufacturers have often struggled to get the recipe right when it comes to the smallest models. They appear to get hung up on a set idea, which can subsequently result in weirdness. The folding Renault Zoom, for instance, with its complex

Yet another bizarre French small car was the 1981 Hrubon, made by Automobiles Schmitt. It was nothing less than a copy of the Mini Moke that appeared to have been squashed to half its normal size. Power came from a Mini engine, and this crazy car was an infrequent sight at French holiday resorts.

MOST
WEDGE-SHAPED

OUT OF 10

9th

The 1972 Tici was a rare British attempt at a truly tiny car. You could build it yourself at home from a kit, using a Mini engine/gearbox, and then attractive young women like this would shun their Rolls-Royce-driving boyfriends and make a beeline for you. You wished.

mechanism to enable it to access the smallest of parking spaces. And the Daihatsu SV250, an essay in narrowness in a world where narrowness isn't particularly important. Volkswagen has consistently demonstrated the ability to create must-have small cars in concept form, the 1991 Chico being a good example, while the latest one, the 1L with its extraordinarily limited thirst for fuel, is another. It is, though, a pity that its showroom-ready small car of the moment, the Lupo, errs so cautiously on the side of convention.

Small cars don't have to be small to be small, if you see what I mean. The 1997 Cadillac Catera is a case in point. A positive dwarf by Cadillac's usual monster standards, the Catera is actually the same size as our very own Vauxhall Omega – a pretty large car on this side of the Atlantic. Giorgetto Giugiaro,

DAFTEST
FEATURES

OUT OF 10

9th

UGLIEST
CAR

OUT OF 10

8th

This boxy little number is the William, a Lambretta powered two-seater aimed fairly and squarely at the miserly country type who was satisfied with nothing more than a feeble chain for a door. It had a single-cylinder two-stroke engine, and a handful, like this one, were imported to Britain in 1972.

The enduring French love of microcars has thrown up some pretty good products. Even former F1 constructor Guy Ligier was drawn into the business, putting his name to a series of minimal motors that were neatly designed and extremely thrifty. This one dates from 1988, and Ligiers are still on sale today.

Small is by no means always beautiful, as this ghastly Riboud Voiturette from 1979 ably proves. Still, with just 47cc in France, no driving licence was needed, it was slow enough for elderly potterers, and could make a gallon of *essence* last an awfully long time. You'd give up long before it did. . . .

CLEVEREST
FEATURES

OUT OF 10

10th

DAFTEST
FEATURES

OUT OF 10

2nd

meanwhile, had his own, individualistic way of designing a small car in the same year. The Italian design maestro was already responsible for the elegant lines of the Lexus GS300, a svelte executive express. His proposal for the Lexus Landau was simply the same car with its golf bag-carrying boot and soberly proportioned nose trimmed off.

You can be sure that, in the face of dwindling roadspace and fossil fuel

The problem of ever-dwindling parking space in our towns and cities was tackled by Renault in 1992 with this concept car called Zoom. The rear wheels folded inwards so the car could be shortened before being inserted into the tightest of spots. It really worked too, but the feature never reached the showroom.

Not every small car is economical in the length department. Daihatsu went for the narrow angle with this zany mid-1980s concept called the SV250. What the point of it was no-one really knew, but at least it used up a smaller amount of the world's resources than most cars.

The 1991 Volkswagen Chico demonstrates its diminutive form next to a Volkswagen Polo, a normal-sized supermini of the time. The Chico looked terrific and bristled with clever ideas . . . yet the tiny VW that did make it to our roads was the disappointingly conventional Lupo.

Put the Japanese, tiny cars, and golf together and this is what you get. The 2002 Suzuki Covie would be the perfect way for two people to get to the golf course – it even has an in-built navigation system – and then play a few rounds, while being as environmentally aware as possible.

The Vauxhall Omega, in a European context, is quite a big car – the sort of thing government ministers and other VIPs swan around in. However, transport it to the USA and it becomes positively cramped, and as the 1997 Catera it became the smallest Cadillac of the 1990s. It was a flop.

Italdesign showed how to make a large car small in 1996 with this, the Landau. It started life as the Lexus GS300, a car originally penned by Italdesign, but then the company chopped off the elegant tail and shortened the well-proportioned nose to create a truncated luxury saloon.

resources, there will be many more interesting tiny cars in the future. Companies such as Japan's Suzuki, besides already manufacturing a large range of compact cars, points the way with novel ideas such as the Covie shown here, a bright and colourful design that positively bristles with consumer-pleasing features. In a few years' time you won't look even slightly bonkers when driving one.

THE VOLVO 480ES
CONVERTIBLE IN DETAIL

Built: 1991 in
Gothenburg, Sweden
Engine: four-cylinder,
1721cc
Top speed: unknown
Sold in the UK? No
Number made: 1

A 'FUN' VOLVO – A CONTRADICTION IN TERMS, SURELY?

The antiques trade swears by them, they line the leafy streets of Golder's Green, and caravans and horseboxes are usually pulled by them. But Volvos have not been, traditionally, fun cars. Before the 1990s, the closest the company has come to glamour is its classic P1800 coupé of 1960. Even then, its stylish image was enhanced by accident: Roger Moore, as TV's *The Saint*, Simon Templar, drove one and instantly made white P1800s chic, but the Volvo was only used because Jaguar refused to lend producer Lew Grade an E-type, 1961's other attractive new car.

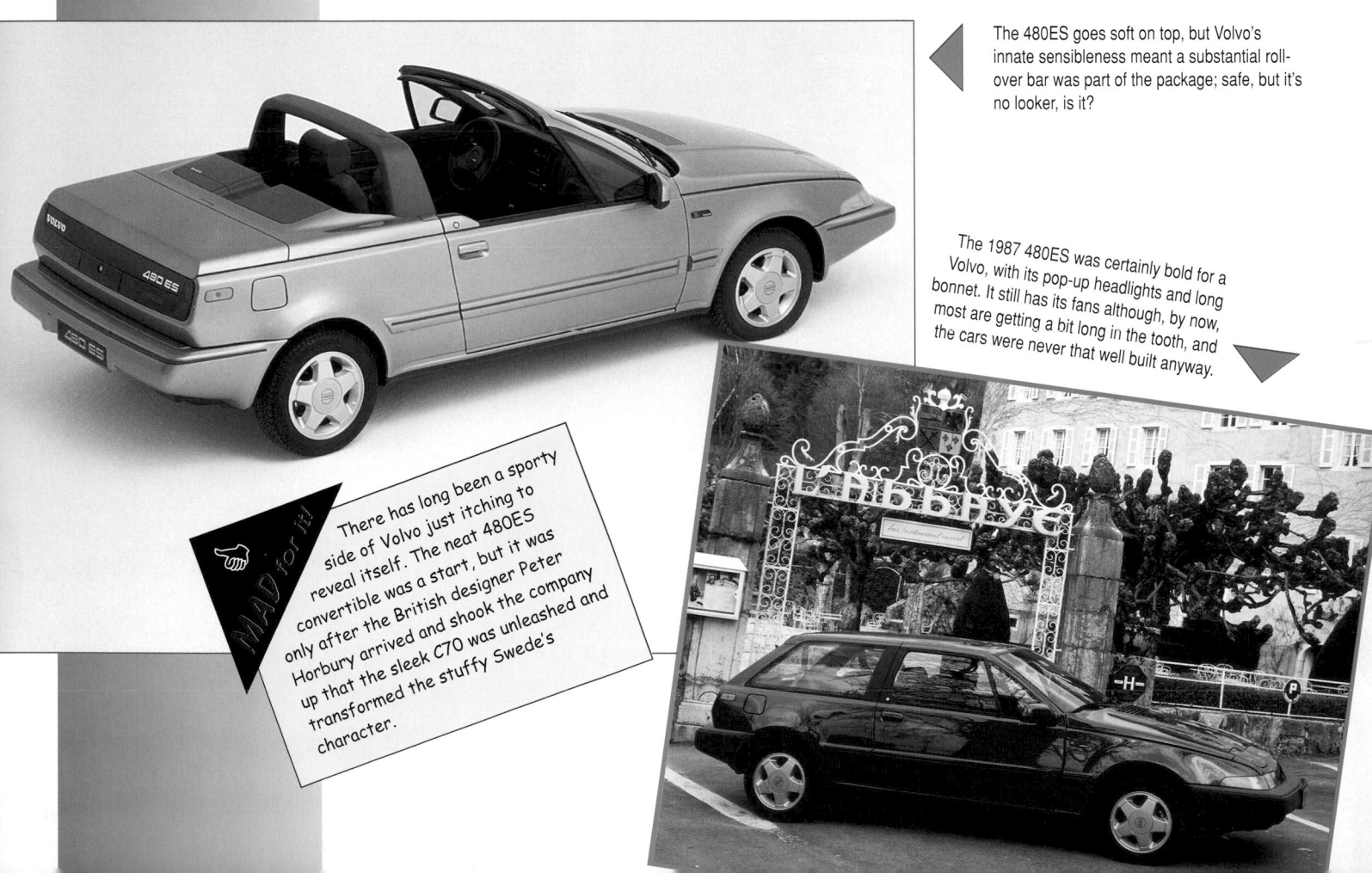

The 480ES goes soft on top, but Volvo's innate sensibleness meant a substantial roll-over bar was part of the package; safe, but it's no looker, is it?

The 1987 480ES was certainly bold for a Volvo, with its pop-up headlights and long bonnet. It still has its fans although, by now, most are getting a bit long in the tooth, and the cars were never that well built anyway.

MAD for it!

There has long been a sporty side of Volvo just itching to reveal itself. The neat 480ES convertible was a start, but it was only after the British designer Peter Horbury arrived and shook the company up that the sleek C70 was unleashed and transformed the stuffy Swede's character.

Volvo's frustrated stylists, though, refused to tow the sombre line. When the eminently sensible 480ES hatchback was unveiled in 1986, they decided to slice the top off to create a two-seater convertible with an electrically operated roof that any young blade would be proud of.

In 1991 Volvo tentatively announced it would go into production but then, feeling perhaps that a convertible was just too frivolous for its sensible nature, the car was cancelled at the last minute, and Volvo PR men hastily changed the subject whenever the matter of Volvo's elusive roadster was raised.

Now, however, a new Volvo coupé and convertible is on sale – the C70. Sideboards, synagogues and showjumpers notwithstanding, Volvo's image has changed forever.

SAD for it! The 480ES itself was an odd-looking beast, with its anteater nose and claustrophobic cabin. Not that well bolted-together either. A ragtop edition, well, that would have been beyond the pale – especially when finished in metallic purple!

In side profile, the Volvo 480ES convertible is neat if unremarkable. The rollbar jars, of course, but the pale purple paint at least lifts the spirits.

Sporty-ish inside, there was no doubt the Volvo 480ES was a tad claustrophobic but, then again, Volvo owners liked that because it gave an atmosphere of tank-like security.

Built: 1938 in Norfolk
Engine: four-cylinder, 747cc
Top speed: unknown
Sold in the UK? No
Number made: 1

HERO OF THE SKIES BUILT HIS DREAM SPORTS CAR FOR SOLID GROUND

Know your Bond films and you'll know who this is towering over the car. No? Ken Wallis ring any bells? Commander Ken Wallis was, in fact, the inventor of the autogyro, a cross between a microlight aircraft and a helicopter. One of these, 'Little Nellie', helped 007 outwit and shoot down his pursuers in *You Only Live Twice*.

MOST SURPRISING

OUT OF 10

10th

Commander Wallis and his dashing Austin Seven Special, its mudguards looking their most rakish and the neatly designed headlamp unit clearly visible between the front wheels.

Here is the father of the autogyro at the wheel: to get that very long bonnet, he used two secondhand Austin Seven chassis welded together.

In this picture, with the Commander safely out of shot and so giving no sense of scale, the Wallis Special looks extremely foppish – like it's driven straight off P.G. Wodehouse's pages.

Before the Second World War, when Wallis was a fearless airborne hero in Lysander and Wellington bombers, his passion was cars. He turned a £25 Bentley 3-litre into a racy two-seater, but this waist-height roadster was his idea of how a perfect rakish sports car should look.

It featured two overlapping Austin Seven chassis, with the end of the front one turned upwards for better steering.

He made the entire body himself from aluminium and, so nothing would spoil its lines, even hid its special French

headlamps behind a curved grille set low between the front wheels.

An ace bomber had no time for such Wooster-ish transport, though, and the car was sold in 1945. What happened to it Wallis never knew. In the 1950s he built

an even more impressive Rolls-Royce-based special, in which he toured the USA while on RAF service.

In 1964 Wallis quit the Force to develop his autogyros full-time. He flew Little Nellie for the stunt scenes in the Bond film and until recently – in his 80s – Wallis regularly took to the air from his home in Norfolk.

THE WEITZ X600 IN DETAIL

Built: 1980 in Wootton, Oxfordshire
Engine: V8, 4949cc
Top speed: unknown
Sold in the UK? No
Number made: 1

MR PERFECT AND THE NIFTY ROADSTER THAT NEVER WAS

John Weitz was among the first men to appear on the International Best-Dressed List in 1967, one of the CV gems making him a sickeningly high achiever. Clothes designer, author of best-selling novels, photographer, ex-US Army Intelligence officer and once accorded Commander rank in the Order of Merit of the German Republic, he splits his time between London, New York and Tokyo presiding over his fashion business.

But his one car design, the X600, was an uncharacteristic low-point in a spangly career; the grand plan to make 1000 replicas never happened.

Berlin-born émigré Weitz was educated at St Paul's School, London and Oxford and was also a keen amateur racing driver. So he chose England as the place to turn his dream car into reality – employing a maker of vintage Bentley copies called Mallalieu at Wootton – in 1979.

The dapper Mr Weitz and his sports car certainly got around the world: here he is in a light drizzle in front of the Imperial Palace gates in Tokyo.

Another city, another pose: Weitz the man and Weitz the car under the Queensborough Bridge in Manhattan, New York – the city where the Weitz fashion empire boomed.

Based on a Chevrolet Camaro Z28 chassis, the swoopy X600 was aluminium-clothed and resembled an Austin-Healey 3000 crossed with the Batmobile. 'I commuted every weekend for six months,' says Weitz, 'Concorde to and fro, to get this thing done.'

But when Mallalieu was wound up after its founder's death, the X600 – intended to sell in the US for $60,000 – went no further. While John Weitz is still at his drawing board at 500 Madison Avenue, X600 lies long forgotten in a Cleveland aircraft museum.

MAD for it! Mr Weitz was a colourful character who couldn't fail to come up with a colourful car. At the time, there were few real sports cars on sale, and the X600 – which Weitz was happy to demonstrate at the drop of a hat – could well have taken the market by storm.

It's June 1980 and John Weitz gives his baby a shake-down at the Lime Rock race track in Connecticut, USA – the car was Chevrolet Camaro-based, yet constructed in Oxfordshire.

SAD for it! The Batmobile was fine for a kid's TV show, but trying to reproduce it on a smaller scale – and without its gadgetry – was always going to produce something a little bit weird. Thankfully for Weitz's considerable bank balance, he decided to keep it as a one-off.

A strange-looking sports car, but there was no doubting its performance; plans to make and sell the X600 for $60,000 a time came to nought.

THE ZAGATO Z-ECO IN
DETAIL

Built: 1992 in Milan,
Italy
Engine: four-cylinder,
899cc
Top speed: unknown
Sold in the UK? No
Number made: 1

HOW TO OWN A BIKE, KEEP IT ON YOUR CAR, AND NOT GET FIT

Fiat knew its baby Cinquecento was spot-on. Why else would it ask eight independent design houses to try and better it? The debut of the new '500' in 1992 was accompanied by a flotilla of specially commissioned 'concept cars' based on its mechanical parts and dimensions. There were the predictable small coupés, buggies and estates, and this curiosity, the Zagato Z-Eco.

Two seats arranged in tandem would take the Z-Eco's occupants to the edge of the city; then one of them could complete the journey on an electric bike. At least, that was the plan. . . .

Venerable Italian coachbuilder Zagato reasoned this would be the ideal car for commuting to work. Its two passengers would sit in tandem under a canopy on one side of the car, as on a motorbike, while an adult-size

To help launch the Fiat Cinquecento in 1992, Zagato was among a posse of coachbuilders and designers who presented their own interpretations of the little city car: theirs was the Z-Eco.

MAD for it! Our towns and cities are grinding to a halt as traffic increases and the means of combating it intensify. So there was some sound thinking in the Z-Eco, half-car, half-bike, as well as proof that Italy's small design companies could come up with real off-beat thinking when given the chance.

Who knows, it could well have been the perfect car for certain individuals, had there ever been a chance it would be made available to the driving, and cycling, public.

The clever part: this is the docking-point where the battery-powered bike would be attached, and through which it would be recharged while the Z-Eco 'mothership' was driving along.

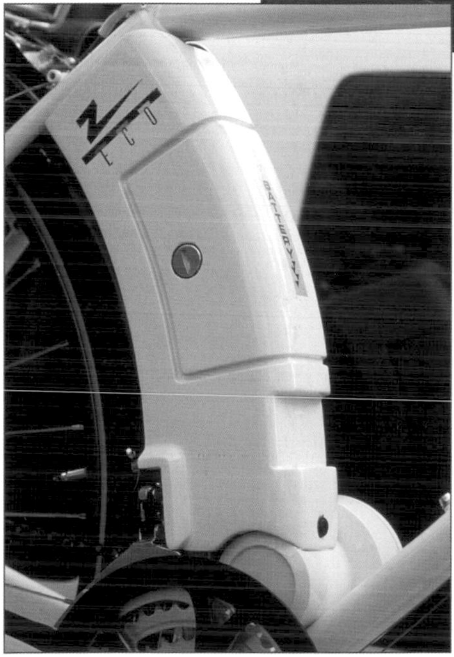

bicycle stood fixed upright on the other. When the traffic ground to a halt, the Z-Eco would be parked in the nearest suburban avenue and one of its occupants would grab the bike and carry on to the office.

MOST USELESS

OUT OF 10

10th

But even that wouldn't be too strenuous because the bike incorporated an electric motor, recharged while on board the car and plugged in, and so ready when needed.

The Z-Eco, though, never turned a wheel – the show car was made of modelling plaster. A shame: getting a bike into a normal Cinquecento was almost impossible.

SAD for it! If you really want to save the planet, keep fit and beat the jams, then you're probably already a walker or a cyclist. If you do fancy a bike then a tandem-seater car to cart it about on somehow defies logic. But can someone please explain what the point of an electric bicycle is?

MAD VANS

If you find you are drawn towards old commercial vehicles, then you'll find yourself in a grubby hinterland halfway between being a car enthusiast and a train-spotter. Let's face it, an interest in old vans and pick-ups is hardly going to make you a big draw at a cocktail party. Still, there is something undeniably appealing about the motoring work-horses that make our lives go round. And I am not talking about the juggernauts that thunder along our roads: I mean the humble delivery vehicles, which are often derived from family saloon cars, that make businesses, both small and large, viable.

My own memories of travelling to London in the back of my father's Ford Escort Mk 1 van, on his regular antiques-buying trips to the city, have undoubtedly given me a rosy view of these contraptions. Wrapped in a blanket and sandwiched between a chest of drawers and a grandfather clock case, there was something very comforting about the clattering roar of this vehicle.

MOST WEDGE-SHAPED OUT OF 10

7th

If you really want your van to say a lot about your company then it might take a bit more than sign-painting. Famous pencil-maker Rowney commissioned this Mercedes-Benz van just after the First World War, to help sharpen up its image, particularly with the royals.

The Ford Escort van, seen here in 1971, is another British favourite, and went through four incarnations before the Fiesta Courier usurped it. On a separate note, just look at the neatness of the landscaping around the AA phone box – and the AA box itself, a relic of the past now we all have mobile phones

A Scammell Mechanical Horse in service, some time in the 1950s, with petrol company National Benzole, for which it's hauling a 750-gallon tanker. These three-wheeled workhorses were once commonplace but today look completely barmy.

Not, of course, that there is anything mad about the Escort. Introduced in 1968, it instantly became a byword for reliable, business transport, rapidly making the market for a small, car-derived van in the UK its very own.

Commercial vehicles, of course, are as old as the automotive industry itself. While the earliest cars were reserved for the super-rich, the other main application of the internal-combustion engine was to power vehicles of commerce. They weren't glamorous, but they helped to make the horse and cart a thing of the past. British company Scammell even went so far as to christen its versatile, three-wheeled delivery vehicle the Mechanical Horse.

This, by today's standards, odd-looking device was once a common sight on British roads, but the nation's army of van drivers do not, as a rule, like to break ranks. Hence, other attempts to interest them in economical, three-wheeled transport have largely failed. The importers of Lambretta's Italian-built, three-wheeled commercials had a

They tried to sell us these little Italian-made delivery vans in the early 1960s, they really did, but British business just wouldn't take them seriously. One wonders how many times the salesman set off in this 'Demonstration Unit' only to return a broken man. Just 200 were sold here, including one to Fortnum & Mason, out of a production run of 71,000.

Here is a 1965 Lancia Superjolly (I kid you not, that really is its name), a front-wheel drive delivery van based on the Lancia Flavia car. Although rarely seen outside Italy, these vehicles were an invaluable extra source of revenue for Lancia, whose cars were beautifully engineered, and so comparatively expensive.

Alfa Romeo's image in 2002 is a carefully nurtured one of race-bred performance and the essence of sexy Italian car design. But when the company was in the Italian state sector it churned out all manner of odd things, including vans that were often converted into police rapid intervention vehicles, and ambulances like this one.

valiant attempt in the late 1950s but made no headway, and Reliant, that bastion of mad British motoring, has recently tried to interest them in a range of Piaggio trucks. You do see one or two pottering around Britain's cities if you look hard enough, but they are still rare.

Italy is perhaps best known for its myriad sports and sporting cars, but even companies like Alfa Romeo and Lancia have made forays into the commercial world. While cars such as the Lancia Flavia and Alfa Romeo Giulietta have tingled the spines of car fanatics, the companies probably made real *lire* from their light commercial vehicles such as the wonderfully named Lancia Superjolly and the eclectic range of trucks and vans bearing the Alfa Romeo name.

The macho, US-style pick-up has never really caught on in the UK – they're too big and thirsty and just not part of any sort of frontiersman culture here. Bedford, though, tried with the 1960 JO, a Bedford J-type cab with a boxy back-end and a Vauxhall Velox engine and interior. It was pretty fast but sales never took off.

Basic in every way, this Standard 10 pick-up was the sort of vehicle your average British window-cleaner or jobbing gardener could aspire to in the 1950s if business went really, really well. At the very least, it would be economical to run, if not especially rugged.

The Felicia Fun was Skoda's 1996 attempt to go all Californian on us, with a hybrid pick-up/convertible aimed at the active outdoor type who likes surfing and beach life, and who could put up with that relentlessly cheerful yellow paint job day in, day out. Here's one beside a deserted English reservoir.

MOST USELESS

OUT OF 10

9th

MOST USEFUL

OUT OF 10

8th

The not altogether unattractive lines of the Subaru Brat pick-up, the most utilitarian but also the most versatile incarnation of the four-wheel drive package that's taken the Japanese firm to the top of the tree in world rallying, and also made the brand a firm favourite with well-to-do country types.

The pick-up is essentially an American confection, an all-purpose vehicle built to withstand any terrain that the United States could throw at it. They're usually too big and too powerful for European markets, but General Motors' Bedford division, a British maker of trucks and vans, did have a try at interesting the British tradesman in a locally produced version. The 1962 Bedford JO united the undoubtedly tough Bedford J-type with the smoothness of a Vauxhall Velox car engine, and even Velox seats, in a package aimed at what it thought were British 'good ol' boys': it was a failure. Your average British window cleaner was probably a little more attracted by

Quite simply, Britain is in love with the Ford Transit. It completely dominates the van market and has done so for decades. It is also now the only Ford-badged vehicle made in the UK. This one is quite mad, the steroid-boosted Supervan II using Cosworth power to turn it into a tarmac-eating slingshot.

something like the 1956 Standard 8 pick-up, which, although spartan, offered excellent economy with useful practicality. But the Brits don't like their utilitarian vehicles any other way: when Skoda tried to market a hybrid convertible/pick-up in the UK, called the Felicia Fun and available only in lurid yellow paint, there were few takers, and even the redoubtable four-wheel drive Subaru Brat was only of interest if all the decals and extras were removed so that it was little more than a practical farmer's friend.

The great British van is perhaps exemplified by the ubiquitous Ford Transit. Indeed, 'Transit Man' has even been identified as a political force in this country, courted and feared by politicians in about equal measure. The Transit was introduced in 1966 and has had the market to itself ever since, despite some competition from Britain's very own Commer, a curiously rounded vehicle once much used by the Post Office. Other American companies have fought shy of marketing vans to the

These strangely rotund Commer vans used to be a common sight in Britain, with their wheels seemingly tucked underneath them like a fat cat's paws. This one, dating from 1959, is every TV licence dodger's nightmare with its elaborate set-detecting paraphernalia provided by Vosper Thorneycroft for the Ministry of Posts and Telecommunications.

Chrysler was one of the pioneers of the multi-purpose vehicle (MPV) in 1983 with its Voyager and Grand Voyager people-carriers, but it also turned the cars into a pair of vans called the Dodge Mini Ram and the Dodge Mini Ram Extended, both of which did sterling service as delivery hacks in suburban America, but were not exported.

It seems amazing that Harrods staff actually built their own electric delivery vans in the 1930s, but it's true. They were in operation for decades afterwards, and the department store even revived them in around 1990 when it commissioned this replica, albeit petrol-powered this time, to keep a tradition alive.

British: Chrysler has managed to interest us in its American-built range of people carriers, such as the present Voyager, but none of its practical delivery vehicles have been sold here.

So we can conclude that the British tradesman is an extremely conservative sort, despite the odd aberration. There can be few businesses like Harrods, which built its own fleet of electric-powered delivery vans in the 1920s and 1930s, in workshops tucked away behind the famous Knightsbridge store. They may indeed today use mostly Transits to deliver their so called 'top people's merchandise' but they did commission a replica of their home-built, iconic vehicle in the 1980s. You might just see it trundling along Brompton Road if you're very lucky.

ten ugliest cars

1. **Beijing** – China's Land Rover, tough as old boots
2. **Dutton Rico** – New outfit for paunchy Escorts gives impression of an ill-fitting suit
3. **Hummer** – Square-rigged brute for ugly situations on the TV battlefields
4. **Kaiser Frazer** – It might have been influential but this one defines the term 'slab-sided'
5. **London Taxi built for Nubar Gulbenkian** – Cab that harks back to the horse-drawn era but is hardly hansom . . .
6. **Nissan Laurel Wessex limousine** – Ghastly '80s saloon is not made any prettier by giving us more of it
7. **Reliant Fox** – Exposed hinges, sliding windows and dumpy looks have never appealed, as this one proves
8. **Riboud** – Pram, golf-cart, shopping trolley and microcar rolled into one wholly unappealing package
9. **Valiente** – Valiant stab at '30s Hollywood glamour not helped by Spitfire centre section
10. **VW 181 'The Thing'** – At least this car is downright ugly on purpose, and has a bohemian image because of it

ten most attractive cars

1. **Avanti** – Timeless sports coupé shape from the man who brought you the Coke bottle
2. **Bentley T Series by Pininfarina** – Italian design adds some slinky sex appeal to Bentley's trad values
3. **Hudson Commodore** – Wheels tucked inside the chassis for this stylish chunk of classic Americana
4. **Karmann Mercedes-Benz 300SL** – Looks like a standard SL until those beautifully designed doors head skywards
5. **Skoda Felicia** – Tricky to drive, possibly, but cool to be seen in with the hood down
6. **Renault Twingo** – Exemplary small car that Renault thought was just too radical for pipe-and-slippers Britain
7. **Rayton Fissore Magnum** – Range Rover, Italian-style that somehow never quite made it as a European 4x4 icon
8. **Ogle SX-250** – Oh-so-chic in 1962 as a one-off, and a hit on the market as the first Reliant Scimitar
9. **Mini** – The last Coopers came loaded with extras but the plain Minis are just as lovable
10. **Timmis** – Painstaking attention to detail has resulted in a dead-ringer for all-time great Ford roadster

1. **Bedford JO** – Britain's very own answer to the all-American pick-up, with loads of power and versatility
2. **Checker Aerobus** – The eight-door, fifteen-seater giant that would be a boon to any airport – or very, very large family
3. **Ford Comuta** – Tiny electric city car – we thought its time had come, thirty-five years late, with Ford's Th!nk
4. **GP LDV** – The beach buggy for anyone who needs to cart the odd fridge back from Dixons
5. **Hobbycar** – Neatly designed amphibian for anyone who wants to sail off into the sunset
6. **Lambretta 175 Commercial** – Nifty three-wheeler that should have set Britain's small businesses abuzz
7. **Steyr-Puch Haflinger** – Pint-sized mud-basher set a trend but was then usurped by the quadbike
8. **Subaru Brat** – Today its Impreza rules the rally roost, but this is how Subaru made its reputation for staying power
9. **Triumph Acclaim** – After years of unreliable rubbish this was BL's first well-built car, with a little help from Honda
10. **UMM** – Tough-as-nails Portuguese off-roader that just begs to be abused

1. **Antique & Classic SS100** – It might look vaguely like a classic pre-war Jag but the clattering VW engine gives the game away
2. **Bentley for HM Queen** – It cost the motor industry £5m to make, but surely something smaller would have done the job
3. **Bond Bug** – No luggage space, seats moulded into place and a clumsy lift-up canopy instead of doors
4. **Ellipsis** – Wheels arranged in a diamond pattern for easy parking and pedestrian kindness, allegedly
5. **Hummer** – Hopelessly wide for use on the road, and you need to be Arnie to master its awful turning circle
6. **Lanchester Sprite** – Waste-of-time design for a famous-named family saloon that could never have been built
7. **Scamp** – Battery-powered shopping car that kind of falls to pieces at the first sign of hard work
8. **Sinclair C5** – Favourite failure of the tabloid press but, then, it was meant for kids to trundle to school in
9. **Skoda Fun** – Bright yellow pick-up that converts into a convertible sun-chaser for those with the ideal lifestyle
10. **Zagato Z-Eco** – Seats arranged in tandem to leave room for an electric bike – but why?

ten cleverest features

1. **Aston Martin DBS V8 by Ogle** – Two rows of lights give followers a clear idea of how hard you're slamming brakes on
2. **Chitty Chitty Bang Bang** – Well it can drive, fly and float – how much more could you ask for?
3. **Chrysler CCV** – Thrifty motor that, claims its maker, is as easy to assemble as an Airfix kit
4. **Cizeta Moroder** – There have only ever been three production V16 engines, and this incredible car possesses one of them
5. **Gatso Flatty** – Knee-high to a grasshopper and a capable race-winner in the hands of the inventor of the speed camera
6. **GP LDV** – Most beach buggies were built for hedonism but, with its useful cargo area, this one has a conscience
7. **Jaguar XKSS** – In this case, clever features included a windscreen and bumpers to 'tame' the D-type for the road
8. **Minissima** – A single door at the back was safe – and proved ideal for wheelchair-bound drivers
9. **Peugeot 402 convertible** – In the late 1930s a folding, all-metal roof was a real piece of motoring theatre
10. **Renault Zoom** – This concept car folds itself up to make getting into tight parking spots a cinch

ten daftest features

1. **Citroën 2CV Metro** – A bigger engine, chrome grille and dummy hood irons don't make a big car out of the 2CV
2. **Daihatsu SV250** – Narrowness in cars had rarely been an issue until this ultra-thin commuter car popped up
3. **Daihatsu Trek** – This car converts into a mobile bivouac for those (fantasy) nights in the wild
4. **Ford Galaxie Thomas Startin hearse** – The very last sort of vehicle in which a race-proven, fire-breathing V8 engine is an advantage
5. **Mercedes-Benz 200 'driverless' car** – A computer takes the hard work out of piloting this experimental machine around a special track
6. **Monotrace** – A two-wheeled car . . . unless you count the two extra wheels needed to stop it from toppling over
7. **Nardi-Giannini 750 Bisiluro** – One part bad, two parts good, or so they thought at Le Mans with this twin-hulled disaster
8. **'Moschino' Rover Metro** – Sorry, Moschino, but black cats and horseshoe decals do not make a trendy car of the Metro
9. **William** – Tiny in every way, but pathetic fencing chains instead of doors to stop you falling out
10. **Wolfrace Sonic** – Six-wheeled whale promoted alloy wheels and terrible pop records

1 **Alfa Romeo 1900 AR52** – No, look again: it isn't a Jeep but a rally-winning Italian off-roader

2 **Hotchkiss-Gregoire** – Front-wheel drive and other advanced features, but the high-technology failed to save Hotchkiss

3 **Isetta** – The archetypal bubble car was also crucial to the fortunes of today's BMW

4 **Lancia Superjolly** – Sharing the mechanical parts with the much-lauded Flavia, this is one delivery van with class

5 **Miele** – Just remember next time you load your German dishwasher that its maker has a car past

6 **Saab Sonett** – It took a while to get the recipe right, but Saab's sports cars went down a treat

7 **Timmis** – A faithful replica that uses some copied bits, some nearly-right parts and some original features of the classic Ford V8

8 **Triking** – Forget everything you think you know about kit cars; this is a finely engineered beauty

9 **Volkswagen W12** – What would the Beetle's planners make of this 200mph 'people's' car?

10 **Wallis Special** – How to weld together two Austin Sevens and come up with a cut-price sports car sensation

1 **Aston Martin Bulldog** – Gullwing doors cause problems in a deluge but the looks are knock-out

2 **Aston Martin DBS V8 by Ogle** – The cigarettes it advertised have vanished but this sleek British supercar has endured

3 **Bond Bug** – Ogle Design's nifty concept very nearly made three-wheelers hip with young drivers

4 **Ikenga** – Under those arrow-like lines lurks a McLaren racing car chassis and lots of original thinking

5 **Minissima** – William Towns' unusual take on the city car theme was much too wacky for stuffy old BL

6 **Nova** – Cut-price Lamborghini needs nothing more than an old Volkswagen to bring it to life

7 **Rowney pencil van** – One characterful delivery vehicle that definitely won't run on unleaded fuel

8 **Sinclair C5** – Single-seater runabout that seemed such a sensible idea until you actually tried it

9 **Tici** – Miniature city car you could build at home and impress the birds with (it was the 1970s, remember . . .)

10 **Vauxhall Equus** – Bold thinking for a new type of British sports car that could so nearly have become wedge-endary

ten most surprising cars   ten most wedge-shaped cars